THE TESTAMENT OF ABRAHAM

THE TESTAMENT
OF ABRAHAM

*Translated from the Greek Text
with Introduction and Notes*

BY

G. H. BOX, M.A., D.D.

DAVIDSON PROFESSOR OF OLD TESTAMENT STUDIES IN THE
UNIVERSITY OF LONDON

WITH AN APPENDIX CONTAINING A
TRANSLATION FROM THE COPTIC VERSION
OF THE TESTAMENTS OF ISAAC AND JACOB

BY

S. GASELEE, M.A.

FELLOW OF MAGDALENE COLLEGE, CAMBRIDGE

WIPF & STOCK · Eugene, Oregon

Wipf and Stock Publishers
199 W 8th Ave, Suite 3
Eugene, OR 97401

The Testament of Abraham
Translated from the Greek Text with Introduction and Notes:
With and Appendix Containing a Translation from the Coptic
Version of the Testaments of Isaac and Jacob
By Box, G. H. and Gaselee, S.
Softcover ISBN-13: 978-1-6667-3474-4
Hardcover ISBN-13: 978-1-6667-9084-9
eBook ISBN-13: 978-1-6667-9089-4
Publication date 9/2/2021
Previously published by SPCK, 1927

CONTENTS

INTRODUCTION

SHORT ACCOUNT OF THE BOOK

The Testament of Abraham, which is quite a distinct work from the *Apocalypse of Abraham*,[1] has been preserved in its original (?) Greek text in a number of MSS. and in two Recensions A critical text of the two Greek Recensions—the Longer (A) and the Shorter (B)—has been edited, with a valuable Introduction, by Dr Montague Rhodes James, together with an Appendix containing in translation extracts from the Arabic version of the Testaments of Abraham, Isaac and Jacob, by Dr. W. E. Barnes.[2] The apocryphon appears to have been translated into a number of other languages (Arabic, Coptic, Ethiopic, Slavonic, Roumanian), and thus clearly enjoyed a certain—if limited—popularity in Christian circles. Dr. James thinks it was written, in its original form in the second century A D, by a Christian writer who used the *Apocalypse of Peter* as one of his sources; its composition is earlier than the time of Origen, but " it embodies legends earlier than that century," and probably " received its present form in the

[1] For this see *The Apocalypse of Abraham*, edited by G. H Box (S P C K , 1918).
[2] Cambridge Press, 1892 (" Texts and Studies," ii 2).

ninth or tenth century," [1] and was written in Egypt On the other hand, both Kohler [2] and Ginzberg [3] emphasize its purely Jewish character—apart from some Christian interpolations—and regard it as an original pre-Christian Hebrew composition, perhaps Essene in character, which was later translated into Greek Kohler, indeed, more recently seems to have modified his original view, speaking of the book as " an Alexandrian product of the first Christian century." [4] The Jewish character of the book will be discussed more fully below, as well as questions concerned with the date of its composition in its original form, and its original language The relation of the two Recensions to each other will also be discussed Meanwhile a brief summary of the contents of the apocryphon may be given Abraham, who is pictured as the hospitable sheikh, ready to welcome strangers and wayfarers, is visited by the archangel Michael, who has been commissioned by God to receive his soul. " The aged patriarch, the friend of God, and benefactor of men, is portrayed as rebelling at first against the fate of mortality, and submitting to it only after having received the promise of being permitted to survey the entire universe before his death Thus he is taken by the archangel Michael in his heavenly chariot to the heights of the firmament, where he looks down upon the earth with its

---

[1] *Test Abrah* , p. 29
[2] *J Q. R* , vii 581 ff
[3] *J E* , i 93 ff
[4] *Heaven and Hell in Comparative Religion* (New York, 1923), p 77.

inhabitants. Then, as he observes the doings of
people, the murder, the adultery, the burglary they
commit, he is horrified, and in his rage he asks the
archangel to smite the malefactors with instant
death, and the archangel is bound to obey. But a
voice from heaven is heard, saying : ' Michael,
chief-captain, bid the chariot to stop, and turn
away Abraham, that he may not see all the world
If he sees all who are living in sin, he will destroy
every existing thing ! For, behold, Abraham has
not sinned, neither pities he sinners; but I made
the world, and will not to destroy any creature from
among them, but I delay the death of the sinner
until he repent and live   Bring up Abraham to the
first gate of Heaven, that he may behold there the
judgements and requitals, and may change his mind
toward the souls of the sinners which he has
destroyed.' "

Dr Kohler [1] thus describes what follows

" God sends Abraham with the archangel to view
Hell and Paradise. A grand scene opens here
before the gaze of the patriarch. Two roads, one
wide and one narrow, stretch on either side, ending
at two gates, correspondingly large and small   A
large procession of souls is led by angels along the
former, and a few walk along the other   In front
of the two gates Adam, of majestic appearance, sits
on a golden throne watching, now weeping and
tearing his hair in distress at the sight of the multitude going through the wide gate, and then smiling
and exulting at the sight of the few entering the

[1] *Heaven and Hell*, p 79.

narrow gate. For while the one leads to destruction and the other to eternal bliss, against seven thousand walking on the road of doom there is hardly one soul walking on the path of righteousness without blemish "

The judgement of souls is further described, and we are told that further on Abraham sees Abel, seated on a crystal throne with a crystal table before him on which is placed an immense scroll wherein the actions of men are recorded by two angels. On the other side two angels are active— one as the weigher of souls, the other as the trier by fire. Abel's position here is explained to Abraham as in accordance with the principle that " man is to be judged by man " (Gen ix. 6). Only at the Last Judgement will God act as Supreme Judge In the case of one soul which the patriarch sees being tested, its good and evil actions are equally balanced. The soul was not to be handed over, in consequence, either to chastisement or salvation, but was to be kept in suspense till the final Judgement Abraham thereupon suggests to the archangel that they should join in prayer on the soul's behalf, which being done, the scale is turned and the soul is led into Paradise

With a fine sense of psychological fitness the writer now represents Abraham as moved by remorse for the fate of the sinners whom in his anger he had consigned to perdition. He invokes the divine forgiveness for their souls, and in answer to his prayer they are restored to life. Abraham is finally brought back by Michael to his home on earth, and the question of his giving up his soul once more arises in an acute form. The Angel of Death is now sent disguised with consummate beauty, and visits Abraham. He at length discloses his identity, and then reveals himself to the patriarch in all his hideousness and corruption. Abraham is still reluctant to give up his soul, but finally Death, taking him by the hand, gradually draws out his soul; he dies and his soul is borne with great honour to Paradise.

It is noticeable that the Testamentary part, which usually forms an essential feature in works of this kind, is absent from our apocryphon We should have expected a dying speech from the patriarch to his assembled family, warning them against certain courses, and giving ethical advice This feature, as a matter of fact, appears in the related writings known as *The Testaments of Isaac and Jacob* which occur in conjunction with the *Testament of Abraham* (see Appendix) Our apocryphon may, possibly, have contained some elements of this kind in its original form, but this is uncertain

TEXT AND VERSIONS

Full details of the Greek MSS of the *Testament* which are known are given by James in the Introduction to his edition (pp I ff). These are ten in number, seven representing the Longer Recension, and three the Shorter "All are late, the oldest belonging, perhaps, to the thirteenth century." The *Testament* usually forms part of a collection of homilies or lives of saints; occasionally apocryphal tracts are included.

There is a tendency shown in some MSS. to abridge, and the text in some passages is corrupt. James thinks the Greek of Recension B is more original and freer from late forms and words than the Greek of Recension A [1] To this point it will be necessary to return in discussing the relation of the two Recensions to each other.

Various secondary versions of the *Testament* (made from the Greek) are in existence, and ought to be mentioned here These are—(1) a Slavonic. An account of this is given by Bonwetsch in Harnack's *Gesch d altchristl Literatur*, I. 914 f There are several texts, and apparently divergent Recensions [2] (2) A Roumanian. This was edited, in text and translation, by Dr. M Gaster, and published in the *Transactions of the Society of Biblical Archæology*, ix 1887 (pp 195–226) The title runs : *The life and death of our Father Abraham the Just, written according to the Apocalypse in beautiful words* It is a form of the Longer Recension, but, in places, abridged (3) An Arabic version, containing the Testaments of Abraham, Isaac and Jacob An account of this is given, with extracts, in translation by Dr. W. E. Barnes in the Appendix to James's ed of the *Testament*. (4) and (5) An Ethiopic and Coptic (for the latter see the Appendix to the present edition) All the three last-mentioned, (3), (4) and (5), present the three Testaments of Abraham, Isaac and Jacob. For the Ethiopic MSS see James, p. 6 f.

The Two Recensions

While the text, especially in some of the secondary versions, has been freely re-handled, especially by

[1] *Op cit* , p 51
[2] For an account of these see *Archiv fur slavische Philologie*, Bd XVIII (1896), pp. 112–125.

way of abridgment, the differences, on the whole,
which represent genuine variations, are to be found
in the two Recensions of the Greek, which are
represented by distinct MSS. On the relation
between the two Recensions, James says, speaking
of the Shorter Recension (B) :

" The language of the narrative throughout is   . simpler
and more antique than that of A   My impression of the
relation of B to A .   is broadly this, that B [i e the Shorter
Recension] preserves the greatest proportion of the original
language, A [the Longer Recension] the greatest proportion of
the original story "

This appears to be a sound inference   It remains
to indicate in broad outline the possible form of
the original story that lies behind the two Recensions. The Longer Recension (A) is certainly more
verbose than the Shorter, but it also differs in details
and in the order of events from the latter (B)
In § 2 B the visit of Michael is somewhat differently
described, in § 3 the speaking tree is in B a tamarisk
with 300 (correct to 331) branches, which is an
original feature, whereas in A the tree is a cypress.
In § 4 B again has preserved an original feature—
the reason for Michael's ascents to heaven, viz. to
lead the angelic choir in its daily song of praise.
In § 7, again, the details of Isaac's dream differ
somewhat in the two Recensions   But the greatest
divergence is reached in the central or apocalyptic
part of the book which treats of the judgement of
souls (A §§ 10–14 = B §§ 8–12). James has summarized these well . [1]

[1] *Op. cit* , p 44 f

" The course of events in A is briefly this

" Abraham on his voyage through the air sees various male-factors, and at his prayer they are destroyed   At God's command he is taken to Heaven, sees the two gates, the two ways, and Adam   Angels are seen driving lost souls, and one soul is seen whose fate is doubtful   A judgement scene is then described, where Abel is judge, an angel, Dokiel, weighs souls, another angel, Puruel, tests them by fire, and two angels act as recorders   The neutral soul is examined, and no verdict given   Abraham intercedes for it and subsequently for the sinners whom he had destroyed, and all are saved   It is explained that every soul will be thrice judged, by Abel, by the twelve tribes .   and by God

" In B we have this

" Abraham is taken to the river Oceanus   The two gates and Adam are seen   Abraham is alarmed, and reassured, on the subject of the narrowness of the gate of life   The lost souls are seen, and one soul of a woman whose fate is doubtful.   The angel who brings them is Death   The judgement scene in Paradise follows   Abel is judge, Enoch is recorder, and two cherubim carry the books of record.   The neutral soul is examined and condemned.   Abraham is taken to the lower firmament, sees the various sinners, as in A, and destroys them   Then he is taken home   All this narrative is in the third person "

The most considerable divergence is in the transposition of the destruction of sinners   Here the position of this episode in A is obviously original   It has been transposed in B for theological reasons—the editor of that Recension evidently thinking it " imprudent to tell men that, though cut off in the blossom of their sin, they might yet escape punishment through the intercession, whether of Abraham or of other righteous men." [1]

Another point in which the two Recensions disagree concerns Sarah; in Recension A she is still alive at the time of Abraham's death, while in Recension B Abraham finds her dead of grief on his return home from the heavenly ride.[2]   In the

[1] James, *op cit*, p 47
[2] According to the Biblical account Sarah had died long before Abraham

concluding sections of the book, which narrate the
visit of the Angel of Death, and finally Abraham's
decease, it is obvious that in Recension B there
has been considerable abridgment. In Recension A
there has perhaps been some amplification here,
especially in the description of the Angel of Death;
but Recension A has preserved the original sequence
of the story. But in one detail Recension B is also
here more original After Abraham has seen
Death in his terrible aspect, he does not fully recover
from the shock, and God removes his soul " as in a
dream " (or " by a kiss," T. B. *Baba bathra 17a*) [1]
Thus the story essentially as it appears in Recension A, with some slight modifications from Recension B, is homogeneous and consistent. While
the Greek of A in course of transmission may have
been assimilated to New Testament language occasionally, and have been expanded or amplified, to
some extent, the substance of the narrative has
not, it would appear, been seriously altered.

The Jewish Character and Origin of the Book

The Jewish character and origin of the book have
rightly been insisted upon by the Jewish scholars
who have made a special study of its contents.
The most important contribution from this side
comes from the pen of Dr. K. Kohler, whose article
published in the *Jewish Quarterly Review* in July
1895 [2] is specially devoted to our book. This has

---

[1] Cited by Ginzberg
[2] " The pre-Talmudic Haggada   II " (Pp 581–606).

been reinforced by Dr L. Ginzberg, who in the *Jewish Encyclopædia* [1] has published his conclusions as to this piece of literature.

The Jewish character of the book is clearly shown by the close and detailed parallels which can be cited from Rabbinic sources An abundance of examples will be found in the notes on the text of the translation that follows, and in the articles by the Jewish scholars cited above Negatively, the absence of specifically Christian elements in the story is remarkable. " In fact," says Ginzberg, " apart from some late Christological additions made in a few MSS by copyists, there is not a single Christian interpolation found in the whole book . . ." The whole tone and framework of the book is Jewish—the rôle played by Michael, the ride in the celestial chariot through the heavens, the peculiar eschatology, all point in this direction. Thus the idea that the representatives of the twelve tribes of Israel shall judge the world (cf Recension A, § xiii.) is thoroughly Jewish, and it is certainly not Christian (contrast Matt. xix 28). In fact so strongly did the Christian copyists feel this that in some of the MSS. a clause is introduced which runs *And at the second coming the twelve tribes shall be judged by the apostles !* [2] In the genuine text of the apocryphon the Messiah as judge does not appear at all, there is, indeed, no mention of the Messiah Adam's fall is nowhere referred to; nor is Death connected in any way

---

[1] Vol I pp 93–96.
[2] Cf. James, *op. cit.*, p 92, critical note (to lines 16–18).

with Satan. He seems to be the embodiment of physical evil

Dr James, who thinks that the book in its original form probably belongs to the second Christian century, and is the work of a Jewish-Christian, regards certain features as distinctly Christian In particular he thinks that the " two ways " and the " two gates " referred to in § xiii are derived from Matt. vii 13 But this is very improbable The idea of the two ways is essentially Jewish, and was known, e g to Jochanan b Zakkai (first century A D), who in the well-known story (T B *Ber*, 28b), as he lay dying, in reply to his disciples' remonstrances because he was weeping, said " *Before me lie two ways, one to the Garden of Eden, the other to Gehinnom, and I know not in which I am to be led* " See further, Century Bible *St Matthew* (ed Box), p 143 (on Matt vii 12–14)

The Jewish character of the apocryphon is further shown by the existence of parallel compositions in Rabbinical literature. Thus there are remarkable resemblances to the *Testament* in a Midrash which deals with the death of Moses, and is extant in a Hebrew form under the title *Pĕtîrath Mosheh*.[1] The general theme of this Midrash is Moses' reluctance to give up his soul. Gabriel and Michael are both requested to perform the task, but without effect. Finally, Sammael, the Angel of Death, volunteers and joyfully departs on his mission, having received the divine permission. He is, however, overwhelmed by the splendour and majesty of Moses' appearance A second attempt when he tries to overawe Moses, but is beaten off with the aid of a staff on which is engraved the Ineffable Name, is equally unsuccessful. Finally, God Himself intervenes, and summons Moses' soul to leave

[1] Jellinek, *B. H.*, vi. 71–78, cf German transl by Wunsche I. 134 ff.

B

his body; the soul is reluctant to do so; and in the end is withdrawn by the divine kiss. Kohler thinks that this Midrash is indebted to the *Testament*. He conjectures that a Midrash *Pĕtîrath Abraham* existed, " if not in writing at least as an oral Haggada. . . ."

Another strongly marked Jewish feature is the description of Abraham's celestial ride above the firmament. This is referred to in the *Midrash rabba* on Gen. xv. 5, where Abraham's experience is interpreted as an ascension to heaven.[1] It is said elsewhere [2] that in order to allow the righteous to die in peace, God makes a preliminary disclosure of the secrets of the other world to them during life.

. . . . .

It may safely be concluded, then, that the book is essentially Jewish in character. Apart from the final doxology and some various readings in the MSS., and some slight traces of Christian influence on the Greek phraseology, there is nothing specifically Christian in the apocryphon. James, indeed, has suggested that the sources of some of the features in the eschatology of the book are to be found in some of the earlier Christian apocalypses, like the *Apocalypse of Peter*. It is far more probable that the eschatology of this and similar writings is ultimately derived from Jewish sources than *vice versa* The dating of its original composition is a difficult problem, the discussion of which must be reserved for a separate section. But in any case

---

[1] Cf. *Ap Abrah*, p xxv
[2] Bereshith *rabba* 62 (cited by Kohler).

it may be regarded as sufficiently early to be entirely free from Christian influence. Why, then, it may be asked, was it so popular in Christian circles? And while it was read in Christian circles, and copied by Christian scribes down to the late Middle Ages, why has it disappeared from the Rabbinical literature? The answer to these questions may be summarized as follows : (a) The story of Abraham's last days was so interesting that it maintained its hold on Christian readers, in its Greek form especially, without difficulty. Abraham is one of the heroes of the Old Testament, and as such occupied a prominent place in the long line of saintly figures of the past. The absence of a Hebrew form of the story from Jewish literature may, perhaps, be explained by the fact that the place assigned to Abraham in our book was occupied in the Rabbinical tradition by Moses. In certain circles of Judaism Abraham came to occupy the central place. Kohler suggests that this was the case in Essene circles. He says :

"We are forthwith introduced into the hospitable tent Abraham had pitched under the oak of Mamre with a view to the four ' high-roads beneath to welcome the rich and the poor, kings and beggars, kinsmen and strangers, as guests ' This feature—prominent also in the life of Job as pictured in *The Testament of Job* and in the Midrash *Aboth de Rabbi Nathan* [1] —occurs throughout the Midrash and Talmud . . It was the Jewish (Essene) system of propaganda still practised by the great mystic Ishmael ben Elisha in the time of Hadrian,[2] and later on adopted by the Christian monks It finds its significant illustration in a tradition preserved by Philo [3] Speaking of *proselytes—gērim*—who ' come over ' from *the path of darkness*

---

[1] Ed Schechter, 33 f.

[2] *Op cit*, § 38, 114

[3] *Monarchy*, 1. 7 · ed Mangey, 11. 220.

and folly to the path of light and truth—he makes Moses enjoin the people not to let these men, who have renounced their country, their kindred and friends, for the sake of joining the true religion, remain destitute altogether of cities, homes and friendships, but to have *places of refuge* always ready to receive them   We arrive here at the very root of proselytism developing from the *hospitium* offered to the *gēr*—the stranger " [1] It is further pointed out, in the same context, that Abraham is, " like a true Essene," pictured as an agriculturist

Whatever view be taken as to its supposed Essene antecedents, it cannot be denied that the book is pervaded by a broad, philanthropic and humanitarian spirit, which would suit Alexandria as its place of origin. Is it a relic of Jewish-Alexandrine literature, originally composed in Greek, and, perhaps, a product of the first century of our era? There are several features which suggest an Egyptian origin for the apocryphon—especially the elaborate description of the Angel of Death, and the weighing of souls.[2]   But these questions must be reserved for fuller discussion below.

THE THEOLOGY OF THE BOOK

In this section some remarks will be made about the angelology and demonology of the book, and its eschatology.

The principal angelic figure is Michael, who still occupies the position of supremacy appropriate to him in the early forms of Jewish religious speculation   The book opens with an account of Michael's commission and visit to Abraham. The fact that Michael, in the first instance, is sent to take the patriarch's soul rather than the Angel of Death, is,

[1] *J. Q. R*, vii 582.   [2] Cf James, p 76.

of course, a signal mark of the divine favour.
Michael also appears (in Recension B, § IV [1]) as
the leader of the angelic choir in heaven, in accordance with Jewish tradition [1] But the most interesting and original conception is that of the Angel of
Death. The monstrous appearance of his outward
form is the subject of an elaborate description
(Recension A, § 17), which is summarized as follows
by James :

" The ground work appears to be the dragon or serpent, with
seven heads, which stands for the seven ages of the world, and
upon this are heaped all the characteristics of the various violent
deaths by which men perish, so that the picture presented to
us is that of a constantly changing Protean figure, turning from
serpent to wild beast, and again into fire, water, sword, poison-
cup and so forth " [2]

This representation is not classical   " The winged
thanatos of Greek art and literature of whom we
read in the *Alcestis*, and whom we occasionally
see in vase-paintings, has nothing monstrous about
him save his wings " The bizarre features, which
do not belong normally to the Jewish Angel of
Death, may be derived from Egyptian sources.
But apart from his monstrous form the figure is
Jewish enough. He is, as Kohler [3] remarks,

" the ancient angel of death as we find him in the Books of
Chronicles, with a few Babylonian and Persian traits attached,
but this ' world-destroyer ' is simply a natural power without
the malignity of the Ahrimanian Satan, and altogether free from
the inherence of sin   He is the personification of physical evil
with its fourteen forms of death, and seventy-two forms of

[1] See notes to the translation of this passage
[2] *Op cit*, p 56
[3] *J Q R*, vii 591 f.

disease,[1] but not of moral evil . He is an agent, not a counterpart of God and of the principle of goodness."

Other angelic beings play a very small part in the book. There are the hostile angels who drive souls (the *malake ḥabbalah*), and the angel Dokiel (= ? " accurate weigher " : Heb. *Dokî'el*) who holds the scales of justice by which the souls (or deeds) are weighed—this conception may well be another Egyptian feature—and the angel who tests by fire— *Purael* (= ? " Fire of God," *i.e.* πῦρ, or possibly " chastiser " = *pur'an+'el*). Further, we hear of good angels casually; but not of demons or devils.

Another interesting feature in an apocryphon, which has an important bearing upon Jewish eschatology, is Isaac's dream narrated in § 7 of both Recensions. The vision, which is not fully and consistently related in either Recension,[2] and which must be reconstructed by a combination of both, refers to the sun, moon, and stars. The sun and the moon are in Isaac's head, and are successively taken away by the Shining One. In the explanation the sun represents Abraham, the moon Sarah, and the stars Isaac's servants : the Shining One is Michael. One mysterious feature is the " rays " of the sun which are left behind with Isaac. According to the explanation given, the rays correspond to the body of Abraham, which is to be left behind in the earth during the twelve hours of the

---

[1] So in the Adam book   cf also the 99,999 diseases of Ahriman

[2] For a discussion of details see James, p 42 f.

day which correspond to the 7000 years which is the period of the world's duration, according to a widely accepted Jewish tradition.

The imagery of the vision is specially interesting, because it is associated with the different degrees of glory shared by the souls of the righteous in Paradise

An important Midrashic passage, given in the name of the famous mystic Simeon B Jochai (*Sifre Debarim*, 10a), teaches that there are " *seven* classes of righteous ones, who will see God's majesty in the world to come, first, ' his loving ones ' are like the *sun ;* the next class like the *moon ,* the third like the *firmament ,* the fourth like the *stars ,* the fifth like the *lightning ,* the sixth like the *lilies ,* and the seventh like the golden candlestick with the olive trees about it " [1] This passage at once illuminates the imagery used by St Paul in the famous chapter of 1 Corinthians about the resurrection (1 Cor xv 41 ff) *There is one glory of the sun, and another glory of the moon, and another glory of the stars , for one star differeth from another star in glory* So also is the resurrection of the dead It is clear that the reference here is to the righteous in Paradise, divided into different degrees of light and glory It is also interesting to note, in this connexion, that the expression " those who love Him (God)" has acquired a special meaning in these contexts It is applied to those who are foremost in piety and righteousness , cf e g the Targum on Judges, v 31 (*But let them that love Him be as the sun when he goeth forth in his might*), which is applied to the righteous in the future world who will shine like the sun, only with light intensified to a strength 343 times as great as it now is (cf Isa xxx 26) The expression *those who love* probably has this technical meaning in such New Testament passages as James 1 12, and 2 Tim iv 8.

A striking feature in the eschatology of this book is the conception of judgement. In § xiii. of Recension A there is a remarkable passage which runs as follows .

Then Abraham said . " My lord chief-captain, who is this judge most marvellous ? . . . The arch-

[1] Cited by Kohler, *J Q R* , vii 597 (ed Friedmann, pp 67 f)

angel answers : *" This man is the son of the first-created Adam, who is called Abel, whom Cain the wicked one slew ; and he sits thus to judge [all creation], trying both righteous and sinners. For God has said : ' I judge you not, but every man shall by man be judged.' For this reason He has given to him judgement to judge the world until His great and glorious advent. And then . . . comes the perfect judgement and recompense, everlasting and irrevocable, which no one can question. For every man has sprung from the first-created, and, therefore, here by his son all are judged. And at the second advent they shall be judged by the twelve tribes of Israel. . . At the third time by the Lord God of all shall they be judged . . .Therefore the judgement and recompense of the world is made by three tribunals "*

Thus there are three judgements · (1) by Abel; (2) by the twelve tribes of Israel, or their representatives; (3) by God finally at the Last Day This certainly appears to be another example of an attempt to combine in one scheme types of eschatology which are fundamentally incompatible. Here the combination includes an individual and a national eschatology; and a temporal and eternal judgement. It is noteworthy that the Messiah does not emerge at any of these points. The second act of judgement (2)—that by the twelve tribes of Israel—corresponds to the advent of the temporary Messianic Age or millennium; but it is a Messianic age without a Messiah

We have a similar combination of incompatible eschatological schemes in the 'Ezra-Apocalypse (cf E A , liv f) As in our apocryphon, the Ezra-Apocalypse combines with schemes of national eschatology one dealing with the eschatology of the individual—the fate of the soul after death (cf 4 Ezra vii 78—100)

The striking episode about the individual soul, whose merits and sins are equal, and whose fate was undecided till Abraham and the angel offered up intercessory prayer on its behalf, calls for remark. The episode is described in § 14 of Recension A. It is remarkable that in Recension B (§ 9), though the neutral soul is mentioned, nothing is said about its being saved by intercessory prayer. It looks as though the author of this Recension regarded the doctrine as dangerous; and it is remarkable that in the Ezra-Apocalypse there is a section (4 Ezra vii. 102—115) which with the greatest emphasis repudiates the idea that there can be any intercession for sinners in the day of judgement. It is clear, however, that in our apocryphon the intercession is intended to apply to the immediate fate of the soul in the intermediate state The final judgement by God is to come, and that will be decisive.

The view that an immediate judgement at death determines the destiny of every man is characteristic of the Jewish Alexandrine theology (see Bousset, *R J*², p. 337 f , and cf *e. g.* Wisdom, iii 1, etc). On the other hand, the eschatology of the *Testament* harmonizes with orthodox Rabbinic theology, which recognized three classes of people who pass at death into the other world, viz. the fully righteous who enter into bliss, the fully wicked who are consigned forthwith to Gehenna, and the large intermediate class (בינונים) who are neither wholly wicked nor wholly righteous. This class—which, of course, includes the large majority—according to the School of Shammai passed for a time (twelve months) into Gehenna to undergo a purgatorial process by fire, and were then released; according to the School of Hillel, however, the divine mercy could be appealed to successfully to mitigate this trial (cf. *Toseft*, Sanh. xiii. 3; T. B. *Rosh ha-shanah* 16 *b*) either by means of the intercession of the fathers, or by the piety of children.[1]

The description (in *Rosh ha-shanah*) runs *They* (the בינונים) *go down into Gehenna, but when they scream* (in prayer) *they are permitted to come up again, as it is written* (Zech xiii. 9) *and I will bring the third part through the fire they shall call on my name, and I shall hear them.*

Volz (p 146) points out that the temporary sojourn of the intermediate class in Gehenna, referred to in this passage, is not to be regarded as taking place in the intermediate state before the Final Judgement, the conception, he thinks, rather is that it follows the Judgement, and is the punishment there awarded. But if this is so, the Judgement must be regarded as taking place immediately after death, and leaves no room apparently for a resurrection. In the *Testament* the reference is plainly and explicitly to the state after death and before the Final Judgement.

There is a curious passage at the end of § xx. (Recension A) where " Abraham's bosom " is referred to; but in its present form the text here is obviously corrupt, as in a speech about Abraham's soul (just after his death) the patriarchs Isaac and Jacob are referred to as being already " in his bosom," *i. e.* enjoying the bliss of Paradise (see note *ad loc*).

Another detail of some interest emerges in § xx. (Recension A) which deserves comment. Abraham's body after death is tended three days. This seems

[1] Cf. *E. A*, p 155.

to reflect the belief that the soul hovers in the neighbourhood of the body for three days immediately
after death, after which it departs to adore God
(see note *ad loc.*).   This idea seems to be earlier
than the notion that the soul has seven days'
freedom immediately after death (cf. 4 Ezra vii. 101).

SOURCES AND LITERARY AFFINITIES OF THE BOOK

The sources of our apocryphon appear to be
entirely Jewish.   Its Jewish character has already
been pointed out, and in view of this fact we must
assume that its sources are to be looked for in Jewish
tradition.

Dr M R James, it is true, is inclined to think that the eschatology of the book has been borrowed from such works as the
Apocalypse of St Peter and the *Apocalypse of St Paul*   But
this view is unconvincing   The resemblances are to be explained
by the view that these apocalypses have themselves drawn upon
earlier Jewish material and tradition   Thus parallels can be
found in the Rabbinical literature for some of the specially
characteristic features of the eschatology, especially traditions
associated with Joshua b Levi (third century A D), who derived
them probably in the last resort from the famous mystic Simeon
b Jochai (end of first half of second century A D) [1]

There are some marked affinities with an apocryphal work, which has survived in a Greek text,
and is known as *The Testament of Job*,[2] which has
been edited by James (*Anecdota Apocrypha*), and also
by Kohler (*Kohut Memorial Vol.*, pp. 264–338).   This
interesting work gives a haggadistic version of the
story of Job, and describes Job's life as one devoted
to the worship of the true God (he, like Abraham, is

[1] See Kohler, *J Q R*, vii.
[2] See *J E*, art "Job, Testament of."

pictured as having been converted from idolatry
in youth), and gives an account of his many trials
and his final prosperity and death. The angels
are represented as coming to take his soul, and just
before his death he delivers an ethical " Testament "
to his children. Kohler regards this work as of
Essene origin

The *Testament* has also some slight relation to
the *Apocalypse of Abraham*, especially to the apocalyptic part, which represents Abraham as surveying
the universe in the heavenly chariot (cf. *Ap Abrah* ,
pp. xxiv ff.). For possible cases of the Testament
influencing later literature, reference may be made
to James, pp. 29 ff   Cf pp. 64 ff.

Date and Original Language of the Composition of the Book

Ginzberg and Kohler (in *J. Q. R*) have argued
strongly in favour of a Semitic original. That a
Hebrew form of the book in some shape originally
existed is highly probable, and that our present
Greek text is ultimately dependent upon this is
also probable   But it must be confessed that the
Greek does not read like a translation.

In favour of its going back to a Hebrew (Palestinian) form is
the peculiar eschatology, which, as has been pointed out above,
is Palestinian and not Alexandrine   Though the present editor
has suggested in a note on the corrupt text in § xix that this
may be explained as due to mistranslation of a Hebrew original,
he lays no particular stress on this suggestion

The story in its original (Hebrew) form probably
grew up in the first half of the first century A D ,
when Enoch had fallen into the background, and

Abraham had become the hero of Jewish legendary lore (cf. Matt. iii. 9), and the " seal of circumcision had become the pledge of life." This probably formed the basis of a free Greek version, which was embellished with some special features (*e. g.* in the description of the Angel of Death) which owed their origin to Egypt (Alexandria)

BIBLIOGRAPHY

A valuable edition of the Greek text of the Longer and Shorter Recensions, with an elaborate introduction, was published in 1892, edited by Dr. M R. James . *The Testament of Abraham the Greek Text now first edited with an Introduction and Notes*, by Montague Rhodes James : with an Appendix containing extracts from the Arabic version of *The Testaments of Abraham, Isaac and Jacob*,[1] by W. E. Barnes (" Texts and Studies " series, Cambridge Press).

Articles by Ginzberg in *J. E* , 1. 93 ff, and by Kohler in *J. Q R* , vii. 581–606 · " The pre-Talmudic Haggada " (July 1895)   see also Schurer, *Geschichte des judischen Volkes* (4th ed), iii, 338 f

An English translation by W. A Craigie is included in the *Additional Volume* added to the " Ante-Nicene Library," and edited by Dr. A. Menzies (1897), pp. 183–201 (the Longer and Shorter Recensions are rendered in parallel columns). The Greek text (based on one MS) has also been printed by Vassiljiv in *Anecdota Græco Byzantina*, t. 1. (Moskau, 1893, pp 292–308) For printed editions of Slavonic and other versions see pp. xi f of the Introduction.

[1] For a Coptic version of these Testaments see the Appendix to the present volume

Short Titles and Abbreviations
used in this Edition

Ap Abr = The Apocalypse of Abraham (ed by G H. Box 1918, published by S P C K)

Apoc N T = The Apocryphal New Testament, edited by M R James (Oxford, 1924)

Beer = *Leben Abraham's nach Auffassung der judischen Sage*, von Dr B. Beer (Leipzig, 1859)

1 Enoch = The Ethiopic Book of Enoch (English translation by R H Charles)

2 Enoch = The Slavonic Book of Enoch (English translation by R H Charles)

Bousset, *R J* [2] = *Die Religion des Judentums*, by W Bousset, 2nd ed , 1906

Jellinek, *B H* = *Beth ha-Midrash* in 6 vols (Vienna, 1859), contains Hebrew text of various minor Midrashim

Lueken = *Michael eine Darstellung und Vergleichung der judischen . . . Tradition vom Erzengel Michael*, von W Lueken (Gottingen, 1898)

Oxford Corpus, ed by Charles = *The Apocrypha and Pseudepigraph of the Old Testament*, ed by R H Charles Vol I Apocrypha , Vol II Pseudepigraph, Oxford, 1913

Pirke de R Eliezer is cited according to the edition (English translation and notes) of G Friedlander (London, 1916)

R. W S [2] = *The Religion and Worship of the Synagogue*, 2nd ed , by W O E Oesterley and G H Box (1911).

Volz = *Judische Eschatologie von Daniel bis Akiba, dargestellt*, von Paul Volz (Tubingen und Leipzig, 1903)

Weber = *Judische Theologie auf Grund des Talmud und verwandter Schriften*, von Dr Ferdinand Weber (Leipzig, 1897)

Wunsche = *Aus Israels Lehrhallen Kleine Midraschim . sum ersten Male ubersetzt*, von Aug Wunsche . 4 vols , Leipzig, 1907–9

D B = *Dictionary of the Bible*

E A = *The Ezra-Apocalypse*, edited by G. H. Box (1912).

J E = *The Jewish Encyclopædia* (12 vols)

J Q R = *Jewish Quarterly Review*.

T. B = Babylonian Talmud

T. J = Jerusalem (or Palestinian) Talmud

THE TESTAMENT OF
ABRAHAM

PART I · THE LONGER RECENSION
(20 Chapters)

Michael's commission. (Chapter I)

I. ABRAHAM lived the span of his life, nine hundred ninety and five years [1] All the years of his life lived he in peace, gentleness and justice, and the just man was exceeding hospitable. He pitched his tent in the four-cross-roads at the oak of Mamre, and welcomed all,[2] rich and poor, kings and rulers, the halt and the weak, friends and strangers, neighbours and wayfarers, that devout, all-holy, just, and hospitable man Abraham did

[1] *Nine hundred*, etc The number fluctuates in MSS , cf the Longer Recension (A has 999 , F 95, which may be a mere scribal error for 995 , but D, E and Ru 175 Rec B has simply *when the days of Abraham's death drew nigh*) The larger number may, however, belong to the older form of the story, and may be due to a free handling of tradition (perhaps (?) to suggest that Abraham, by living to within five years of 1000 [= 1 day] had partially retrieved the sin of Adam which led to his dying at the age of 930 [= 1000 − 70])

[2] *welcomed all* This representation of Abraham as the hospitable sheikh may be illustrated elsewhere in Jewish literature , see Introduction, pp xix f

C

welcome equally.   The bitter cup of death that
cometh to all inexorably, even the unforeseen end
of his life, overtook him too.   Now the Lord God
called his archangel Michael, and spake unto him .
Michael, chief-captain,[1] go down to Abraham,
and tell him concerning his death, that he shall take
order for the settling of his temporal estates : for
I have blessed him as the stars of the heaven, and
as the sand that is beside the sea-shore.[2]   He liveth
in abundance of much substance and great estates,
and he is exceeding rich.   But above all else, he is
just with all goodness, hospitable and loving kindly,
even unto the end of his life.   Do thou, archangel
Michael, depart to Abraham, my well-beloved
friend, and tell him concerning his death ; give him
this assurance : " In this season thou art destined
to depart from this vain world, and shalt quit the
body, and thou shalt come unto thine own Master
among the righteous."

The archangel visits Abraham and, after a time, discloses his errand.   Abraham is reluctant to give up his soul.   (Chapters II–IX)

II. The chief-captain went out from the presence
of God, and went down unto Abraham to the oak
of Mamre, and found the just man Abraham very
nigh unto the place, sitting by the yokes of oxen for

---

[1] *chief-captain* (ἀρχιστράτηγε)   This accords with the representation of Michael in Rev xii 7   He is styled " chief-captain " in the Slavonic Enoch xxii 6, xxxiii 10   cf also LXX of
Daniel viii 11

[2] Cf Gen xxii 17

tillage, with the sons of Masek [1] and among others his servants, twelve in number. And behold, the chief-captain was coming towards him. Then Abraham seeing the chief-captain Michael coming from afar, like unto a most glorious warrior, rose up and went to meet him, as was his wont, advancing to meet all strangers and welcoming them. Then the chief-captain saluted him first and spake unto him : Hail, most reverend father, just soul, chosen of God, true friend of the Heavenly One. Abraham said unto the chief-captain : Hail, most reverend warrior, beaming as the sun, all-glorious, above all the sons of men. Thy arrival is well-timed ! Wherefore I beseech thee by thy presence whence hath come the youth of thy years ? Tell me, thy suppliant, whence, from what host, and from what journey hath come thy beauty ? Then said the chief-captain ; I, just Abraham, am come from the great city ; from the great king have I been sent to take the place of a true friend of his, for the king doth summon him. Abraham said : Come hither, my lord, with me, as far as my place. The chief-captain said : I come. Then went they and sat them down to converse in the place of the tillage. Abraham said to his servants, the sons of Masek : [1] Go ye to the drove of horses and take two horses tame, and gentle, that have known the bit, that we may sit thereon, this stranger guest and I. Then the chief-captain said : Nay, my lord Abraham, let them not bring horses, for I abstain therefrom,

[1] *the sons of Masek* So the MSS The true reading should be *the son of Masek*, i e Eliezer, cf Gen xv 2 (LXX)

even from ever sitting upon a four-footed beast.
Is not my king rich in great possessions, having
authority both over men and all manner of beasts
of burden? Yet I abstain therefrom, even from
ever sitting upon a four-footed beast. Let us
depart, then, O just soul, on foot, walking gently
until we reach thy house. And Abraham said:
Amen, so be it.

III. Now as they were going from the field to
his house, along that road stood a cypress tree,[1]
and at the bidding of God the tree spake with a
human voice, and said: Holy, holy, holy, is the
Lord God who is summoning him to (be with) those
that love him[2] And Abraham hid the mystery,
for he thought that the chief-captain had not heard
the voice of the tree   Then came they nigh unto
the house and sat them down in the court   And
Isaac saw the face of the angel, and said to Sarah[3]
his mother: My lady mother, behold, the stranger
that sitteth with my father Abraham is no son of
the race of those that dwell on the earth. Then
ran Isaac, and did obeisance to him, and fell at the
feet of the spirit.[4]   And the spirit[4] blessed him and
said: The Lord God will freely grant thee his
promise which he promised thy father Abraham

---

[1] According to Rec B the tree was a tamarisk tree which
had three hundred (and thirty-one = אשל *tamarisk*, which by
Gematria = 331) leaves, cf Gen. xxi 33   For the rustling of a
tree regarded as an oracle, cf 2 Sam v 24

[2] *him*, i.e Abraham   *to be with those who love him*, i e with
the just in Paradise, cf James, i 12; I Cor ii 9

[3] *Sarah* by a sort of anachronism is regarded as still living—
another case of free handling of tradition

[4] *the spirit*, lit " the incorporeal one " (τοῦ ἀσωμάτου)

and his seed, and he will grant thee freely even the
precious prayer of thy father and thy mother.
Then Abraham said to Isaac his son: Isaac, my
son, draw water from the well and bring it to me in
the bason that we may wash the feet of this stranger.
He is weary, for he hath come unto us after a long
journey. Then ran Isaac to the well and drew water
in the bason, and brought it to them. Then Abraham came nigh and washed the feet of the chief-
captain Michael, and the bowels of Abraham were
moved, and he wept upon the stranger. And Isaac
saw his father weeping and himself wept too, and
the chief-captain saw them weeping and wept
with them, even himself with them; and the tears
of the chief-captain fell upon the bason into the water
of the vessel, and they became pearls of wondrous
value. And Abraham was astonished when he
saw the marvel and took the stones secretly, and
hid the mystery, keeping it with himself alone in
his heart.

IV. Then spake Abraham unto Isaac his son:
Depart, my beloved son, into the reception chamber,[1]
and adorn it   spread there for us two couches, one
for me, and one for the guest here who is sojourning
with us to-day. And get thou ready for us there
a large seat [2] and a lamp-stand and a table with
abundance of every good thing. Adorn the chamber,
my son, and unfold fine cloths, purple and linen.[3]

---

[1] Greek, εἰς τὸ ταμεῖον τοῦ τρικλίνου   Michael is treated as a
royal visitor
[2] Greek, δίφρον
[3] Greek, σινδόνας καὶ πορφύραν καὶ βύσσον

Burn every precious incense of high repute, and take sweet-smelling herbs from the garden, and fill our house therewith. Kindle seven lamps full of oil, that we may make merry,[1] for the guest here who is sojourning with us to day is more glorious than kings and rulers, for even his appearance surpasseth all the sons of men. Then Isaac made ready all things well, and Abraham took the archangel Michael by his side, and went up into the reception chamber; and they both sat them down on the couches, and between them he brought forward a table with abundance of every good thing. Then the chief-captain arose and went outside, as if by constraint to ease himself, and ascended into heaven [2] in the twinkling of an eye, and stood before the face of God and spake unto Him Lord and Master, may it please thy might to know that I cannot akill to announce to that just man the mention of death : I have not seen upon the earth his like, pitiful, hospitable, just, true, god-fearing, abstaining from every evil deed. Now know, Lord, that I cannot akill to make mention to him of death. Then said the Lord: Go down, Michael, chief-captain, to my friend Abraham, and whatsoever he says unto thee, that do thou even do. if he eateth, do thou too eat with him. And I will send

---

[1] The kindling of many lights was a sign of feasting and joy, cf 4 Ezra x 2 Lights are so used, and are a prominent feature in the Jewish Feast of Dedication (called also " Festival of Lights ") cf *R W S* [2], p 404

[2] According to Rec B, Michael ascends to heaven at sunset, at the time when the ministering angels sang their hymn of praise in heaven before God, and when the archangel must needs be present as their leader

my holy spirit upon his son Isaac, and will cause
the mention of his death to enter into the heart
of Isaac, that even he may see in a vision the death
of his father, and Isaac will tell the vision and thou
shalt interpret it, and he, even Abraham, shall
recognize the end thereof. Then said the chief-
captain. Lord, all the heavenly spirits lack bodies
They neither eat nor drink [1] This man spread at
my side a table with abundance of all the good substance of the earth that perisheth. Now, O Lord,
what shall I do? How can I escape his notice,
sitting at one table with him? The Lord said:
Go down to him and take no thought with thyself
concerning it While thou art sitting with him
I will send upon thee an all-devouring spirit, and he
shall consume all that is on the table, from thy hands
and through thy mouth.[1] Be thou merry with him
in all things. Only thou shalt interpret fairly the
truth of the vision, that Abraham may recognize
the sickle of death, and the unforeseen end of his
life, and make order for the settling of all his worldly
possessions, seeing that I have blessed him above
the sand of the sea and as the stars of the heaven

V Then the chief-captain went down into the

---

[1] Cf Luke xxiv 39, 43 For the idea that angels could not
eat cf Tobit xii 19 The conception was widespread and well
known (cf the Patristic comments on the visit of the three
Angels to Abraham) It was generally supposed that the
" eating," when it apparently took place, was in appearance only;
cf the Tobit passage cited above, and also Josephus, *Anti*, i 11 2,
and Philo, *De Abrahamo*, § 23, *Midrash rabba* Genesis xlviii 14
Here, however, the food and drink are really consumed by " an
all-devouring spirit ", cf with this view Justin Martyr, *Trypho*,
§ lvii, where the eating of angels is compared with the eating of
fire.

house of Abraham, and sat with him at the table,
and Isaac ministered unto them.   Now when supper
was finished, Abraham made his wonted prayer [1]
and the archangel prayed with him, and they rested,
each on his couch   And Isaac spake unto his
father . Father, I too would fain have seated with
you on this couch, that I too also may hear your dis-
course, for I love to hear the excellence of the conversation of this all-virtuous man.   And Abraham
said : Nay, my son, but depart to thy chamber and
rest upon thy bed, that we may not be too wearisome
to this guest   Then Isaac received his blessing,[2] and
blessed him, and departed to his own couch, and
fell upon his bed   And God caused the mention
of death to enter into the heart of Isaac as in dreams.
And about the third hour of the night Isaac awaked
from sleep and rose from his couch and came running
to the chamber where his father was sleeping with
the archangel   So Isaac knocked quickly at the
door, saying . Arise, father Abraham, open unto
me quickly, that I may enter and hang upon thy
neck and salute thee ere they snatch thee up from
me.   So Abraham arose and opened unto him,
and Isaac entered and hung upon his neck, and began
to weep with a loud voice.   And the bowels of Abra-

[1] Abraham is here represented as reciting a prayer (or prayers)
like a pious Jew before retiring to bed for the night   The custom
was old (cf T B *Berak.* 4b)   For the forms of such prayers in
present use cf Singer, pp 293–7
[2] The blessing of children by parents has always been a
prominent feature in the domestic life of the Jews, and is attested
in the ancient sources   In later Jewish custom it was usual for
the children to be blessed by the father on all important occasions,
notably on Sabbath eve and the holidays   See further the
article " Blessing of Children," in *J E* , iii 242 f.

ham were moved with him, and he too wept with a
loud voice. And the chief-captain saw them weeping and wept himself too   And Sarah, who was in
her tent, heard their weeping and came running unto
them, and she found them embracing one another
and weeping. And Sarah said with weeping : My
lord Abraham, what is this, that thou weepest ?
Tell me, my lord, has this brother here, who is
sojourning with us to-day, brought thee news
concerning thy nephew Lot, that he has died ? and
is it for this that ye weep thus? But the chief-
captain broke in upon her, and said unto her · Nay
Sister Sarah, it is not so, as thou sayest, but methinks,
thy son Isaac saw a dream and came unto us weeping,
and we saw him, and our bowels were moved in
pity with him, and we wept.

VI. When Sarah heard the excellence of the
conversation of the chief-captain, she straightway
recognized that the speaker was an angel of the
Lord. So Sarah beckoned Abraham to go without
towards the door, and said unto him : My lord
Abraham, knowest thou who this man is ? And
Abraham said : I know not. Then said Sarah :
Thou knowest, my lord, the three men, the heavenly
ones, who sojourned in our tent beside the oak of
Mamre,[1] when thou didst slay the calf without
blemish and set a table by their side; and when
the meat had been eaten the calf rose again and
sucked its mother in great joy. Knowest thou not,
my lord Abraham, that they gave unto us Isaac
according to their promise, even the fruit of my

[1] Cf Gen xviii 1-10

womb? Of those three holy men this is one. Then
spake Abraham : O Sarah, this is truth that thou
hast spoken. Praise and glory from God even the
Father. Yea, even I, in the late evening, while
I was washing his feet in the bason of the vessel,
said I in my heart : These are the feet which I once
did wash among the three men. And later, his
tears fell in the vessel and became pearls of great
price. Then took he them from his bosom and
gave them to Sarah, saying · If thou believest me
not, now behold these. And Sarah took them and
did obeisance, and clung fondly to them, and said
Glory be to God who sheweth unto us wonders.[1]
Now know, my lord Abraham, that a revelation
of some event is among us, whether it be evil or
good.

VII. And Abraham left Sarah and went in to
the chamber and said unto Isaac   Come, my beloved
son, tell me the truth; what were the visions and
what didst thou experience, that thou camest
running unto us ?   Isaac cut him short and began
to speak : I saw, my lord, in this night, the sun
and the moon [2] above my head, and the rays thereof,
encircling me, and giving me light. As I was thus
beholding them and enjoying (the sight), I saw the

---

[1] This is rather like a Jewish form of Benediction   cf Ber
ix 1   *Blessed art Thou, O Lord our God, King of the Universe,
who hast wrought miracles*, etc   To ejaculate such an acknow-
ledgment in the presence of some wonderful experience is a
thoroughly Jewish practice, see further *J E*, iii 8 ff , s v.
Benedictions

[2] *sun and moon*   For the symbolism (sun and moon in a
dream symbolizing father and mother) cf. Gen xxxvii 9 (Joseph's
dream)

heaven open, and saw a man bearing light coming down from heaven and flashing more brilliantly than the beams of seven suns. Then that man, like unto the sun in visage, took the sun from off my head, and went up into the heavens where he had come down. And I was exceeding grieved for that he took the sun away from me. And after a little, while I was still grieving and lamenting, I saw that man a second time coming down from heaven. And he took away from me the moon also, from off my head. And I wept exceedingly and cried unto that man light-bearer, and said: Do not, my lord, do not take away my glory from me; pity me and hearken unto me, and even though thou hast taken away the sun from me, spare me yet the moon. But he said   Let them be taken up to the king that reigneth above, for he would fain have them there   And he took them away from me, but spared to me the rays. Then spake the chief-captain: Hearken, just Abraham. The sun, which thy son hath seen, thou art, even his father, and the moon likewise is his mother Sarah. The man who bore light, who came down from heaven, he is the messenger from God, who is destined to take thy just soul from thee. Now know, most reverend Abraham, that thou art destined in this season to leave the life of the world and migrate unto God. Then said Abraham to the chief-captain: O most novel of marvels ! Indeed now, art thou he who is destined to take my soul from me ? The chief-captain said unto him   I am Michael, the chief-captain, who standeth in the presence of

God,[1] and I have been sent to thee to put thee in remembrance of thy death. This done I shall return to Him as we were bidden. Abraham said : Now know I that thou art an angel of the Lord, and thou wast sent to take my soul. Nevertheless I will not follow thee; but do as thou art bidden.

VIII. The chief-captain heard this word and straightway vanished from sight. He went up to heaven and stood in the presence of God, and told all that he saw in the house of Abraham This word also spake the chief-captain to the Lord · Even thus saith thy friend Abraham I will not follow thee; nevertheless do as thou art bidden. Now, O omnipotent Lord, doth thy glory and thy deathless dominion command aught? Then God spake unto the chief-captain Michael : Go down to my friend Abraham yet once again and speak thou unto him · Thus saith the Lord thy God, who brought thee into the land of the promise, who blest thee above the sand of the sea and above the stars of the heaven, who opened the womb of Sarah the barren, and blessed thee with Isaac, the fruit of the womb, in old age : Verily I say unto thee, that blessing, I will bless thee, and multiplying, I will multiply thy seed, and I will give unto thee all the

[1] Throughout this apocryphon Michael occupies the chief place in the angelic hierarchy, the part that is elsewhere assigned to Metatron As such he here describes himself as the angel " who stands in the presence of God," i e the celestial being who has immediate access to the presence of God, the " Prince of the Presence " (sar ha-panim), which is Michael's original title " before he is transformed into the Metatron " (Ginzberg) According to 2 Enoch xxii 6, it is Michael, " the chief-captain," who brought Enoch " before the face (presence) of the Lord " See further, Ap Abrah (ed Box) pp xxv f

boons thou askest of me, for that I am the Lord thy God, and beside me there is none other. But tell thou me why thou art withstanding me, and why is grief within thee?   And why art thou withstanding my archangel Michael?   Knowest thou not that all who are (sprung) from Adam and Eve have died? Yea, none of the prophets hath escaped death : and none of those who rule is immortal; neither hath any of thy forefathers escaped from the mystery of death.   All have perished, and all have made their peace in the grave—all are gathered in by the sickle of death.   But against thee I have not sent death, neither have I allowed deadly disease to overtake thee.   I have not permitted the sickle of death to overtake thee, neither have I allowed the snares of hell to enmesh thee : never did I will thee to meet with any harm.   But for good comfort have I sent my chief-captain Michael to thee, that thou mayest know thy departure from the world, and make disposition concerning thine house and concerning all thy estates, and that thou mayest bless Isaac thy well-beloved son.   Now recognize that I have done thus desiring not to grieve thee. Wherefore then saidst thou to my chief-captain : I will not follow thee?   Wherefore hast thou thus spoken?   Knowest thou not that if I give leave to Death, and he cometh upon thee, thus I should see whether thou wouldest come, or whether thou wouldest not come?

IX. Then the chief-captain took the exhortations of the Lord, and went down unto Abraham; and when the just one saw him he fell upon his face to

the ground as one dead; [1] and the chief-captain
told him all that he had heard from the Most High.
Then did the holy and just Abraham rise up with
many tears and fell at the feet of the spirit,[2] and
besought him saying : I beseech thee, chief-captain
of the powers above, since thou hast deigned to
come thyself altogether unto me a sinner and thine
all-unworthy servant, I implore thee even now, O
chief-captain, to be the medium of my word yet
once (again) unto the Most High, and thou shalt
say unto Him · Thus saith Abraham, thy servant,
O Lord God . [3] In every deed and word which I
have asked of thee thou hast heard me, and hast
fulfilled every desire of mine   Now, O Lord, I
resist not thy might, for I also know that I am not
immortal but mortal   Even so, to thy command,
all things yield, and shudder, and quake at the
presence [4] of thy might, so I too.   Yet one boon ask
I of thee.   Now, Lord God,[5] hear my request ,
while I am yet in this body, I would fain see all the
world and all created things which thou didst
stablish together, through one word,[6] O Lord, and
when I have seen these, then cheerfully will I depart
from life   So the chief-captain departed again,
and stood in the presence of God and told him all,

---

[1] Cf *as one dead*, Rev 1 17, 4 Ezra x 30 , and for the representation cf Dan viii 17, 18 , x 9, 10, 15.

[2] Lit the incorporeal one

[3] Greek Κύριε κύριε = perhaps אדני יהוה , cf Ezek. xxxix
17 (LXX)

[4] Cf 4 Ezra viii 20 f

[5] Gk. δέσποτα κύριε   cf LXX, Gen xvi 2, etc.

[6] *by one word*   This is the older view (cf Ps xxxiii 6)   The
later Rabbinical view was that Creation was effected by ten
words   cf *Pirke Aboth*, v 1.

saying . Thus saith thy friend Abraham   I would fain behold all the world in my life, before I die When the Most High heard this request, he again commanded the archangel Michael, and said unto him : Take a cloud of light and those angels that bear command over the chariots, and go down, and take the just man Abraham on a chariot of the cherubim and exalt him into the air of heaven so that he may see all the world.

Abraham enters the Divine Chariot and rides through the Heavens. (Chapters X–XIV.) [1]

X. Then went down the archangel Michael, and took Abraham upon a chariot of cherubim, and exalted him into the air of heaven, and led him with sixty angels on the cloud, and Abraham went up on the chariot over all the earth   And Abraham saw the world just as it was that day . [2] some ploughing, others driving wains : in one place shepherds tending flocks, and in another, watching in the fields by night; men dancing, sporting, playing the lyre; in one place wrestling and pleading, in another, weeping; and then saw he the dead held in memory by monument.   And he beheld too the newly-wedded being escorted,[3] in a word,

---

[1] The mystical experience which enabled those who had been initiated to enter the heavenly sphere, and penetrate the secrets of the universe, was often pictured as a ride through the heavens in the divine chariot (see *J E*, vii 499 f *seq*)   In *Ap Abr* Abraham is described as ascending to heaven with the archangel on the wings of birds (chap xv)

[2] Cf *Ap Abr*, xxi ff

[3] *being escorted*, i.e   in   the   marriage   procession   (Greek ὀψικευομένους)

saw he all that was going on in the world, good and evil. So Abraham, as he went through [the air], saw warriors bearing swords, wielding in their hands whetted swords; and Abraham enquired of the chief-captain : Who are these? And the chief-captain said : These are robbers, who intend to murder and steal, and burn, and destroy And Abraham said : Lord, Lord, hear my cry and bid that wild beasts come forth from the thicket and devour them. And even as he uttered (the word) there came forth wild beasts from the thicket, and devoured them. And in another place saw he a man with a woman committing fornication with each other, and he said : Lord, Lord, bid that the earth open and swallow them up And immediately the earth opened and swallowed them up In another place he beheld men digging through an house, and robbing the goods of others, and he said : Lord, Lord, bid that fire may come down from heaven and devour them.[1] And at his word, fire came down from heaven and devoured them Then straightway came a voice from heaven [2] to the chief-captain, thus saying : Michael, chief-captain, bid the chariot to stop, and turn away Abraham, that he may not see all the world. If he sees all that are living in sin, he will destroy every existing thing.[3] For behold, Abraham has not sinned, neither pities he sinners; but I made the

[1] Cf 2 Kings i 10, Luke ix 54 f
[2] The " voice from heaven " corresponds to the Rabbinic *bath ḳol*, see art " Voice " in Hastings' *D C G*
[3] Greek ἀνάστημα = Heb *yĕḳûm*, cf Gen vii 4, 23 (LXX and Hebrew).

world, and will not to destroy any creature from among them, but I delay the death of the sinner, until he repent and live. Bring up Abraham to the first gate of heaven, that he may behold there the judgements and the requitals, and may change his mind toward the souls of the sinners, which he hath destroyed.

XI So Michael turned the chariot, and brought Abraham to the east, to the first gate of heaven [1] And Abraham saw two ways, the one way narrow and compressed, and the other broad and spacious, [2] and there also he saw two gates, one gate broad on the broad way, and one gate narrow on the narrow way. And outside the two gates there I [3] saw a man seated upon a golden throne, and the appearance of that man was terrible, like unto that of the Lord. And I saw [3] many souls being driven by angels and led in through the broad gate; and other souls I saw,[3] few in number, that were being borne

[1] For the various " gates " of heaven cf 4 Ezra iii 19 (with the note in *E A* , p 14 f)   Michael turns the chariot to the east, where Paradise was situated (cf 2 Enoch xlii 3, and 1 Enoch xxxii 1f)

[2] Cf Matt vii. 13 f , 4 Ezra vii 3 ff   The figure of the two ways, one leading to life, and the other to death, occurs in the *O T* , cf Jer xxi 8 (Deut xi 26, xxx 15), Prov xxvi 18, and appears to have become a stereotyped idea in Jewish literature well before the Christian era   When R Jochanan b. Zakkai (end of first century A D) lay dying, he wept, and on being asked why, said   " Before me lie two ways, one to the Garden of Eden, and the other to Gehinnom (Gehenna), and I know not in which I am to be led " (*T.B Berak* , 28b)   See further, Box on St Matthew vii 13 f (Cent. Bible, new ed), and Strack-Billerbeck, *ad loc*

[3] Or " they saw," Greek ἴδον   The first person may be more original   For the change from first to third person see XII (beginning) note.

D

by angels through the narrow gate [1]   And when the marvellous being who sat upon the golden throne saw few entering in through the narrow gate, but many entering through the broad gate, straightway that marvellous man did pluck the hairs of his head and the sides of his beard, and hurled himself on the ground from his throne, weeping and wailing. And when he saw many souls entering through the narrow gate, then he arose from the ground and sat upon his throne, rejoicing and exulting with great jubilation.   Then Abraham asked the chief-captain : My lord, chief-captain, who is this all-marvellous Man, who is adorned with such majesty, and sometimes weeps and wails, and sometimes rejoices and exults?   The spirit [2] said : This is Adam, the first-created man,[3] who is in such majesty, and he beholds the world, for all are sprung from him ; and when he sees many souls entering through the narrow gate, then he rises and sits upon his throne, rejoicing and exulting jubilantly, because this narrow gate is that of the just, which leads unto life, and these that enter through it, enter into paradise   And therefore the first-created, Adam,[3] rejoices, because he sees the souls being saved But when he sees many souls entering through the broad gate, then he plucks out the hairs of his head, and hurls himself on the ground, weeping

---

[1] Cf *Pirke R Eliezer*, XV   The angels who drive and scourge the sinful souls through the broad gate are the " angels of destruction " (*malākê ḥabbalah*, Eccles   Rabba iv 3) or " angels of Satan " (*malake Saṭan*, Tosef   *Shabb* , xvii 3), pitiless and fierce of aspect

[2] Greek ὁ ἀσώματος (" the incorporeal one ")

[3] Greek ὁ πρωτόπλαστος Ἀδαμ (" the Protoplast Adam ")

and wailing bitterly. For the broad gate is that of sinners, which leads to destruction and to everlasting punishment. Wherefore the first-created, Adam,[1] falls from his throne, weeping and wailing for the destruction of sinners, for many are they that are perishing but few they that are being saved.[2] For in seven thousand scarce is there to be found one soul saved, that is righteous and undefiled.[3]

XII. And while I was thus speaking,[4] lo, two angels fiery in visage, and pitiless in intent, and harsh in looks, were even (now) driving on a thousand souls, pitilessly beating them with fiery lashes[5] And one soul the angel seized. And they drove all the souls into the broad gate towards destruction. So we also followed the angels, and came within that broad gate, and in between the two gates stood a throne, dread in appearance, of dread crystal, flashing like unto fire, and upon it sat a wondrous Man, shining as the sun, like unto the Son of God. Before him stood a table like crystal, all of gold and fine linen. And upon the table was lying a book, the thickness thereof six cubits, and the breadth thereof ten cubits,[6] and on the

---

[1] Greek ὁ πρωτόπλαστος Ἀδαμ ("the Protoplast Adam")

[2] Cf Matt xxii 14, 4 Ezra viii 3 ("Many have been created, but few shall be saved") The fewness of the saved is the theme of 4 Ezra vii 49–61

[3] For the thought cf 4 Ezra ix 21

[4] Note the change from the third to first person, which is common in this type of literature The first person may be more original

[5] Greek χαρξαναῖς = "lashes" or "chains"

[6] In Zech v 1, 2, the "flying roll" which contains the divine curses (cf Ezek ii 9, iii 1–3) is ten cubits in breadth (as here), here the thickness (six cubits) is given, but not the length These measurements are designed to suggest immense size

right hand thereof and on the left stood two angels, holding paper, and ink, and pen. And before the table sat an angel light-bearer,[1] holding in his hand a balance,[2] and on the left sat an angel, fiery, altogether pitiless and harsh, holding a trumpet in his hand, which contained within it all-devouring fire to test the sinners And the marvellous Man who was seated on the throne, himself judged and gave sentence to the souls. And the two angels on the right hand and on the left recorded. The one on the right hand recorded the righteousnesses, and the one of the left the sins. And the one before the table, who held the balance, weighed the souls ; and the fiery angel, who held the fire, tested the souls. Then Abraham asked the chief-captain Michael : What is this which we behold ? And the chief-captain said : These things which thou seest, holy Abraham, are the judgement and recompense. And behold the angel who was holding the soul in his hand, brought it before the judge. And the judge said : Open me this book and find me the sins of this soul. And he opened the book and found its sins and its righteousnesses equally balanced, and he gave it neither to the testers nor to the saved, but set it in the midst.

XIII. Then Abraham said : My lord chief-

---

[1] Greek ἄγγελος φωτοφόρος (φωτοφόρος = Lucifer)

[2] Cf Ezra iii 34 (" weigh our iniquities   in the balance "), also 1 Enoch xli 1   The metaphor of " weighing " good and bad deeds (merits and sins) against each other is common in the Rabbinic literature, cf e g *Pesikta* xxvi (ed Buber, 167a). *R Eliezer says   the scales are evenly balanced—the scale of iniquities on the one side, and of merits on the other , the Holy One inclines (the balance) to the scale of merit.*

captain, who is this judge, most all-marvellous?
and who are the recording angels? and who is the
angel, like unto the sun, holding the balance? and
who is the angel, the fiery one, holding the fire?
And the chief-captain said: Seest thou, most holy
Abraham, the dread Man that sits upon the throne?
This Man is the son of the first-created Adam who
is called Abel, whom Cain, the wicked one, slew;
and he sits thus to judge all creation, trying both
righteous and sinners. For God has said: I judge
you not, but every man shall by man be judged.[1]
For this reason He has given to him judgement,
to judge the world, until his great and glorious
advent. And then, O righteous Abraham, comes
the perfect judgement and recompense, everlasting
and irrevocable, which no one can question   For
every man has sprung from the first-created,[2]
and therefore here first by his[3] son all are judged.
And at the second advent they shall be judged by
the twelve tribes of Israel,[4] both every spirit and

[1] Based on Genesis ix 6 (" whoso sheddeth man's blood, by
man," etc , i e as the Palestinian Targum interprets it, the
murderer will be condemned by judicial process , in other words
man shall be judged by man).

[2] The protoplast Adam

[3] his, i e Adam's son, viz Abel, the first martyr

[4] Kohler (J Q R , VII 586 f) suggests that the text has
been altered here   He thinks it may have originally run, " And
at the second advent [of the great Ruler] to the twelve tribes,"
etc   This is very unlikely   As the text stands there are three
judgements, viz (1) by Abel, (2) by the twelve tribes of Israel,
(3) by God finally   This looks like an interesting attempt to
combine the eschatology of the nation with that of the individual
(the two being really incompatible, in this form)   The idea of
the world of mankind being judged by the twelve tribes of Israel
(contrast Matt xix 28, where the tribes are judged) is thoroughly
Jewish, cf e g Sibyll Oracles, iii 781 (the Israelites " judges

every creature. At the third time, by the Lord God of all shall they be judged; and thereupon the end of that judgement is near, and dreadful is that sentence, and there is none to release   Thereupon the judgement and recompense of the world is made through three tribunals. And therefore a matter is not finally established by one or two witnesses, but every matter shall be established by three witnesses   And the two angels,[1] the one on the right, and the one on the left, these are they which record the sins and the righteousnesses. The one on the right hand records the righteousnesses, and the one on the left the sins. And the angel who is like unto the sun, holding the balance in his hand, is Dokiel,[2] the archangel, the just holder of the balance, and he weighs the righteousnesses and the sins with the righteousness of God. And the fiery and pitiless angel, who is holding in his hand the fire, this is the archangel Puruel,[3] who

and righteous kings of mortals ")   For the idea of the specially righteous judging the twelve tribes, cf *Test* xii *Patriarchs*, *Judah*, xx 5   Cf also the Yalkut on Daniel, § 1065   " In the time to come the Lord will sit in judgement, and the great of Israel will sit on thrones prepared by the angels, and judge the heathen nations, together with the Lord " (cited by Ginzberg)   Cf. also *Sifre*, 131a to Deut xxxii 1, and see further Volz, p 343

[1] For the recording angels cf 2 Enoch xix 5   In *T B Hag* 16a two angels of service are referred to which " lead " a man, these are said in the Talmudic passage to " witness against him " Ginzberg suggests that these two angels are meant here, who " officiate temporarily as recorders during the judgement " If so they would change presumably with each individual judged   The permanent recorder is Enoch, " the scribe of righteousness "

[2] *Dokiel* = Heb **דוקיאל** i e " exact weigher "—the archangel who holds the scales of justice

[3] *Puruel* looks like a Græcized form (from πῦρ, fire) of Uriel = " Fire of God "   cf *E A*, p 20. For the weighing of souls and their purification by fire see Introduction, p xxii.

has authority over the fire, and tests the works of men through fire. And if the fire shall burn up the work of any man, straightway the angel of judgement takes him and carries him away into the place of sinners, place of punishment most bitter; but if the fire shall try the work of any man without laying hold upon it, this man is justified, and the angel of righteousness takes him and carries him up to be saved in the lot of the just. Thus, most just Abraham, all works among all men are tried by fire and by the balance

XIV. And Abraham said unto the chief-captain : My lord chief-captain, the soul which the angel was holding in his hand, why was it sentenced to be set in the midst ? [1] Then said the chief-captain · Hear, just Abraham. Because the judge found that its sins and its righteousnesses were equal, so he committed it neither to condemnation nor to be saved, until what time the judge of all shall come Abraham said to the chief-captain : What is lacking to the soul for it to be saved? The chief-captain said : If it win one righteousness over and above its sins it enters into salvation. Abraham said to the chief-captain · Come hither, chief-captain Michael, let us make a prayer on behalf of this soul, and see if God will hearken unto us. [2] The chief-

[1] For this expression, " in the midst," in this connexion cf the Rabbinical term for a soul that is neither completely righteous nor completely wicked, viz *bĕnôni*, i e " one in between " See further Introd , pp xxv f

[2] The idea that the merit of the righteous (especially righteous Abraham) avails much, and particularly in intercession, is strongly marked in this passage, cf Gen xviii 23 ff (Abraham's intercessions for Sodom), Ep James v 16 In 2 Enoch vii 4

captain said : Amen, so be it   Then they made prayer and supplication on behalf of the soul, and God heard them; and when they rose up from their intercession, they no more saw the soul standing there.   And Abraham said to the angel : Where is the soul which thou didst hold in the midst? And the angel said   It has been saved by thy righteous prayer, and behold, an angel light-bearer has taken it and carried it up into Paradise.   And Abraham said . I glorify the name of the most high God and His unfathomable mercy :   And Abraham said to the chief-captain : I pray thee, archangel, hear my supplications, and let us yet again call upon the Lord and supplicate His pity and beseech His mercy upon the souls of the sinners whom I once with evil purpose cursed and destroyed, and the earth swallowed up, and the beasts tore to pieces, and whom the fire devoured through my words.   Now know I that I have sinned before our Lord God.   Come, Michael, chief-captain of the hosts above, come, let us call upon God with tears that he may forgive me my sin, and grant them unto me.   And the chief-captain hearkened unto him, and they made supplication before God.

(cf also 1 Enoch xiii 4, xv 2) Enoch as a righteous man is asked by the fallen angels to pray and intercede for them   In our passage the value of intercession for the dead is implied, which was later embodied in the custom of children praying for dead parents, and by their prayers delivering them from punishment, cf Marmorstein, *Doctrine of Merits*, pp 44 and 156 f   In 4 Ezra vii 102–115 the idea that any intercession can avail in the final day of judgement is expressly repudiated. In *Apocalypse of Moses*, xxxiii , the angels make intercession for Adam just dead

When they had called upon Him for a long time a
voice came from heaven saying : Abraham, Abraham, I have hearkened unto thy voice and thy
supplication, and I forgive thee thy sin, and those
whom thou thinkest I did destroy, them I have
recalled, and have led into life by my extreme
goodness. Because for a season I have requited
them in judgement   For those whom I destroy
living upon the earth, in death will I not requite
them.[1]

Abraham returns to his house ; he refuses to yield up his soul.   (Chapter XV.)

XV. And the voice of the Lord said also unto
the chief-captain : Michael, Michael, my Minister,
turn back Abraham to his house, for behold his
end is at hand, and the span of his life is fulfilled,
so that he may make disposition concerning every-
thing,[2] and then do thou take him and bring
him unto Me. So the chief-captain turned back
the chariot and the cloud, and brought Abraham
to his house   And departing to his chamber he
sat him down upon his couch. And Sarah[3] his
wife came and embraced the feet of the spirit,[4]
and spake as a supplicant, saying : I give thee

[1] Such a death would atone for offences previously committed
Cf The Mishnah *Sanh* vi 2 and the Gemara on the passage
[2] Cf 2 Kings xx 1.
[3] Note that Sarah is here represented as still alive, in Rec B
(XII), on the other hand, she is found dead of grief by Abraham
on his return home   Both recensions disagree with the Biblical
account, according to which Sarah died many years before
Abraham
[4] Greek τοῦ ἀσωμάτου (ὁ ἀσώματος)

thanks, my lord, that thou hast brought back my
lord Abraham; for behold we thought he had
been taken up from us   Then came Isaac his son
and fell upon [1] his neck; and in like manner all
the men-slaves and women-slaves surrounded Abraham and embraced him, glorifying God.   And the
spirit [2] said unto him · Hearken, righteous Abraham,
behold thy wife Sarah, behold too thy beloved son
Isaac, behold too all thy men-servants and maid-
servants arrayed about thee.   Make disposition
of all thy possessions, for the day is at hand in which
thou art destined to depart from the body, and once
again to come unto the Lord   Then said Abraham ·
Has the Lord spoken, or dost thou of thine own
will say these words ?   Then said the chief-captain
Harken, righteous Abraham , the Lord has commanded, and I tell it unto thee   Then said Abraham . I will not follow thee.   The chief-captain;
when he heard this word, straightway went out
from the presence of Abraham and went up to the
heavens, and stood in the presence of God the Most
High, and said . Lord Almighty, behold, I have
harkened unto Thy friend Abraham in all that he
has said unto Thee, and I have fulfilled his petition.
I have shown to him Thy dominion and all the
land and sea beneath heaven.   I have shown to him
judgement and retribution through a cloud and a
chariot; and again he says I follow thee not   And
the Most High said unto the angel, Is it even so
that again my friend Abraham says thus, I follow
thee not ?   And the archangel said . Lord Almighty,

---

[1] Lit " embraced "   [2] Greek (ὁ ἀσωμάτος)

thus he says, and I refrain from touching him, for from the beginning he is Thy friend, and all things pleasing in Thy sight he has done; neither is there any man like unto him upon the earth, no, not even Job [1] the marvellous man. Wherefore I refrain from touching him. Command then, Immortal King, what shall be done.

The Angel of Death visits Abraham.
(Chapters XVI–XVII)

XVI. Then said the Most High : Call me hither Death, who is called the shameless face and pitiless glance. So Michael the spirit [2] went away and said unto Death, Come hither, the Lord of Creation, the Immortal King, calls thee Death, when he heard, shuddered and trembled, possessed with great cowardice, and he came with great fear, and stood before the unseen father, shuddering, groaning, and trembling, awaiting the command of the Lord So the unseen God said to Death Come hither, thou bitter and cruel name of the world, hide thy fierceness, veil thy foulness, and cast off thy bitterness from thee,[3] and gird around thee

---

[1] Job, as is traditional, is represented as a contemporary of Abraham and the patriarchs In the apocryphal *Testament of Job*, Job is represented as saying in his farewell address to his children that he was a descendant of Esau, and belonged to the generation of Abraham In the Mishnah (*Sotah*, v 5) the question of the nature of Job's piety is referred to, whether he was primarily a lover or merely a fearer of God Like Abraham, Job, according to the *Testament*, had changed from idolatry to the worship of the true God

[2] Greek ὁ ἀσωμάτος

[3] " The disguise is considered necessary lest Abraham, as Moses did after him, might drive death off at once by using the power of the Holy Name " (Ginzberg).

thy youth and all thy glory, and go down to Abraham my friend, and take him and lead him to me. Yet even now command I thee not to terrify him, but take possession of him with coaxing, for he is my very friend. When Death heard this, he went out from the presence of the Most High and girded about him a most glorious robe, and made his countenance like unto the sun, and became comely and blooming, passing the sons of men, having assumed the form of an archangel,[1] with his cheeks flashing like fire, and he went away unto Abraham. Now the righteous man Abraham (had) emerged from his chamber and was sitting beneath the trees of Mamre, holding his chin in his hand,[2] and was expecting the coming of the archangel Michael. And behold, a smell of sweet savour came to him, and a flashing of light, and turning round, Abraham saw Death, coming towards him in great glory and comeliness. And Abraham rose up and went to meet him, for he thought he was the chief-captain of God, and seeing him Death did obeisance to him, saying : Hail,[3] honoured Abraham, righteous soul, true friend of the Most High God, and companion of the holy angels ! And Abraham said unto Death, Hail,[3] thou that appearest and in form art as the sun, most glorious helper, light-bringer, marvellous man, whence comes thy glory unto us, and who art thou, and whence hast thou come ? So Death said : Most righteous Abraham, behold, I tell thee the truth.

[1] It is possible that St Paul alludes to this legend in 2 Cor xi. 14 ("Even Satan fashioneth himself into an angel of light")
[2] "The conventional attitude of dejection" (James)
[3] So Rec B (XIII), reading χαῖρε   text here has χαίροις

I am the bitter cup of death [1] Abraham said to him :
Nay, but thou art the fairness of the world, thou
art the glory and the beauty of angels and of men,
thou art more comely than every form, and sayest
thou *I am the bitter cup of death,* and not rather,
I am more comely than every good thing ? But Death
said : I speak the truth unto thee, what God has
named [2] me, that I tell thee   And Abraham said :
Wherefore hast thou come hither? And Death
said : For thy holy soul am I come.   Then Abraham
said : I know what thou meanest, but I will not
follow thee.   And Death was silent, and answered
him not a word.

XVII. Then Abraham rose up and went to his
house, and Death too followed him thither. And
Abraham went up into his chamber, and Death
went up with him   And Abraham reclined upon
his couch, and Death came and sat beside his feet.
And Abraham said : Depart, depart from me, for
I am minded to rest me on my couch.   Death said :
I depart not until what time I take thy breath from
thee   Abraham said unto him : By the immortal
God I charge thee speak unto me the truth.   Art
thou Death ?   Death said unto him : I am Death :
I am he that blights the world.   Abraham said :
I pray thee, since thou art Death, tell me, comest
thou thus unto all in such comeliness, glory, and
fairness ?   Death said · Nay, my lord Abraham;

---

[1] *the bitter cup of death ,* i e " the poison of death " (Heb.
sam ha-māweth), an allusion to the name of the angel of death,
Sammael (cf the Jerusalem Targum to Gen iii 6 : *and the
woman beheld Sammael the angel of death*).

[2] i e the name Sammael, as explained above.

for thy righteousnesses and the measureless sea of
thy hospitality, and the greatness of thy love
towards God have become a crown upon my head,
and in beauty, and in great peace and winsomeness
come I to the righteous, but to sinners I come in
great corruption and fierceness and very great
bitterness, and with a fierce and pitiless [1] glance.
Abraham said . I beseech thee, harken unto me,
and show me thy fierceness, and all thy corruption
and bitterness. Death said : Thou wilt not be
able to behold my fierceness, most righteous Abraham. Abraham said · Yea, I shall be able to behold
all thy fierceness, because of the name of the living
God,[2] for the power of my God which is in heaven
is with me. Then Death put off all his beauty and
fairness, and all his glory, and the form that was
like unto the sun, wherewith he was clad, and girded
about him his robe of tyranny, and made his countenance gloomy,[3] and fiercer than all manner of
wild beasts, and more foul than every kind of foulness; and he showed Abraham seven fiery serpents'
heads, and fourteen faces,[4] of the most burning fire,

[1] The representation of the aspect of the Angel of Death as
" fierce and pitiless," which is a constant feature in these descrip-
tions, was probably suggested by the name *Azazel* (interpreted
as a compound of *'azaz,* ' rough,' ' fierce,' and *'el*), who plays the
part also of Sammael

[2] *i e.* the power which Abraham possessed of using the ineffable
Name would protect him from possible fatal consequences

[3] For a parallel description of the terrible faces of Death see
T B *Al-zara,* 20*b* (cited in the additional note, p 90).

[4] The " seven fiery serpents' heads " correspond to the seven
ages of the world (7000 years), see Rec B, Chap VII and note
The " fourteen faces " appear to be as follows (1) fire, (2)
darkness, (3) viper, (4) precipice, (5) asp, (6) lion, (7) cerastes,
(8) basilisk, (9) fiery sword, (10) lightning and thunder, (11)
sea, (12) river, (13) three-headed serpent, (14) poison-cup

and of great fierceness, and a countenance like unto
darkness, and a most gloomy countenance of a
viper, and a countenance of a most horrible precipice,
and a countenance fiercer than an asp, and a countenance of a dread lion, and a countenance of a
horned serpent (cerastes) and of a basilisk   He
showed him too a countenance of a fiery sword,
and a scimitar-bearing countenance, and a countenance of lightning that flashed forth lightning
fearfully, and an echo of fearful thunder.   He showed
him too another countenance of a fierce, billowy sea,
and a fierce river plashing, and a monstrous three-
headed serpent, and a wine-cup mingled with
poisons; and in a word, he showed him great fierceness and bitterness unendurable, and every deadly
disease as of the odour of death.   And from the
great fierceness and bitterness there died servants
and maid-servants in number about seven thousand
And righteous Abraham came into a deadly faintness,[1] so that his spirit failed him.

Intercession for those who have died at the presence of the Angel.   (Chapter XVIII)

XVIII. When the all-holy Abraham had thus
seen these things he said to Death . I beseech thee,
all-destructive Death, hide thy fierceness, and gird
about thee thy beauty, and the shape which thou
hadst before.   Straightway Death hid his fierceness

---

[1] Greek $\mathring{\eta}\lambda\theta\epsilon\nu$ $\epsilon\mathring{\iota}s$ $\mathring{o}\lambda\iota\gamma\omega\rho\acute{\iota}\alpha\nu$ $\theta\alpha\nu\acute{\alpha}\tau o\upsilon$? " came into indifference
of death " ? a physical sensation of weariness, produced by the
shock, is meant

and girded about him his beauty which he had before. And Abraham said to Death : Why hast thou done this, that thou hast slain all my men-servants and maid-servants ?   Did God for this purpose send thee hither to-day ?   Death said : Not so, my lord Abraham, it is not as thou sayest, but on thy account was I sent hither.   Abraham said to Death : How, then, have these died ?   Has not the Lord commanded it ?   Death said : Believe, most righteous Abraham, that this also is marvellous, that thou also wast not carried off with them.   Yet speak I unto thee the truth   For if the right hand of God had not been with thee in that hour, thou too wouldest have had to depart from this life.   Then said righteous Abraham : Now I know that I have come into a deadly faintness, so that my spirit fails.[1] Yet, I beseech thee, all-destructive Death, since my servants have died untimely, let us beseech here the Lord our God, that He will hearken unto us and raise up them that have died untimely through thy fierceness.   And Death said : Amen, so be it.   So Abraham rose up and fell upon the face of the earth and prayed, and Death with him.   And God sent a breath of life upon the dead, and they were quickened with life.   Then the righteous Abraham gave glory unto God.

[1] For this representation, which is common in apocalyptic writings (the prostrating effect of the vision or appearance of the angel), cf. Daniel viii 17, x 8, 16, Ezek i 28, iii. 23, xliii. 3, Rev i. 17, 4 Ezra x 29, *Ap Abraham* x (beginning). Here, however, the reference is more particularly to the paralysing effect produced by the sight of the Angel of Death in his fierce natural aspect. The " terrors of the Angel of Death " are described in T. B. *Abodah zarah*, 20b (see p 30 *n*).

The Interview continued.   (Chapter XIX)

XIX. And going up into his chamber he lay down , and Death came also and stood before him. And Abraham said unto him : Depart from me, for I am minded to rest because my spirit is in (a state of) weariness. Death said · I depart not from thee until I take thy soul And Abraham, with harsh countenance and angry glance, said to Death : Who has commanded thee to say this ? Thou sayest these words of thyself boastfully and I will not follow thee [1] until the chief-captain Michael come to me and I shall go away with him, yet even this do I tell thee   If thou desirest that I follow thee, explain unto me all thy changing shapes—the seven fiery heads of the serpents, and what means the countenance of the precipice, and what the sharp sword, and the raging river, and the turgid tempestuous sea. Teach me too concerning the unendurable thunder and the fearful lightning, and what was the ill-savouring cup mingled with poisons Teach me concerning all   And Death said : Harken, O righteous Abraham, for seven ages [2] do I ravage the world, and drive down all into hell, kings and rulers, sick and poor, slaves and freemen, do I send to the depth of hell   Therefore showed I thee the seven heads of the serpents. And the

---

[1] So in the Midrash, which describes the death of Moses, when Sammael, the Angel of Death, confronts him with the demand for his soul, Moses drives the angel away with the staff on which is engraved the divine name   see Introd , p xvii

[2] i e presumably the seven ages during which the world endures   cf T B Sanh , 97a, " six thousand years shall the world continue, and in the seventh it shall be destroyed "

E

countenance of the fire I showed unto thee because many are burned to death by fire, and through the countenance of fire they see death.   The face of the precipice I showed thee, because many men die coming down from high trees or fearful cliffs, and swoon [1] and die,[1] and they see death in the shape of a fearful precipice.   The face of a sword I showed thee because many fall by the sword in wars, and see death in a sword.   The face of a mighty surging river showed I to thee because many are snatched away by a flood of many waters, and are carried off by very mighty rivers, and are choked and die, and see death untimely.   And the face of the rude, rough sea I showed thee because many are shipwrecked in a sea by a mighty wave and are overwhelmed, and see death as the sea.   And the unendurable thunder and the fearful lightning I showed thee because many men,[2] when they encounter a season of (divine) wrath, at the onset of unendurable thunder and fearful lightning suffer violent death, and thus behold death [as unendurable thunder and fearful lightning].[2]   I showed thee also venomous

---

[1] Gk ἀνύπαρκτοι γινόμενοι

[2-2] The whole passage, which is obviously corrupt, runs in Greek as follows . [διότι πολλοὶ τῶν ἀνθρώπων] ἐν ὥρᾳ θυμοῦ τυχόντες βροντῆς ἀνυποφόρου καὶ ἀστραπῆς φοβερᾶς ἐλθούσης ἐν ἁρπαγῇ ἀνθρώπων γίνονται καὶ οὕτως τὸν θάνατον βλέπουσιν.   As it stands it yields no satisfactory sense.   In particular ἐν ἁρπαγῇ ἀνθρώπων is a very curious expression   If it can be assumed to have arisen from a mistranslation of a Hebrew original, this might be restored בהמם מתים, mĕthîm = " dead " or " die," being confused with mĕthîm = ἀνθρώπων   With this emendation the sentence can be made to yield a sense that harmonizes with the context, the general idea being that certain men who meet with a violent death are victims of the divine wrath because they are sinners, and deserve swift punishment   cf Luke xiii 4

beasts, vipers and basilisks, leopards and lions, and lions' whelps and bears, and vipers—in a word, I showed thee the face of every wild beast, most righteous one, because many men are made away with by wild beasts, while others, being breathed upon by venomous snakes, serpents and vipers, and horrid reptiles and basilisks, breathe their last. I showed thee also deadly cups filled with poison because many men are given poisons to drink by other men, and in a moment unexpectedly are carried off.

Abraham's Death and Departure to Paradise.
(Chapter XX.)

XX Then said Abraham : I beseech thee tell me : is there an untimely death ? Death said : Verily, verily I say unto thee as God's truth there are seventy-two deaths.[1] One is the just death that has its allotted time.[2] And many men (there are who) within one hour [3] go to death, and are consigned to the grave. Behold, I have told thee all thou hast asked. Now say I to thee, most just Abraham, put away every device,[4] and leave thy questioning once and for all, and come follow me

---

[1] *seventy-two deaths* cf. *Apoc Moses*, xxxiv (Charles, *Apocryph. and Pseudep*, II 142), according to which Adam was afflicted with seventy or seventy-two " strokes " or ailments, which resulted in his death. The number seventy or seventy-two symbolizes what is comprehensive or complete, cf. Steinschneider, *Z D M. G*, LVII. 474–507.

[2] Gk ὅρον

[3] *i e* suddenly, without much warning

[4] Gk πᾶσαν βουλήν

as the God and judge of all has commanded me.
Abraham said to Death : Depart from me yet a
little while, that I may rest on my couch, for I am
in great despondency. Ever since I have seen thee
with my eyes my strength has failed me, and all the
limbs of my flesh are as a weight of lead, and my
breath labours distressfully. Depart for a little,
for I have said, I cannot bear to see thy form. Then
came Isaac his son and fell upon his breast weeping.
And his wife Sarah,[1] too, came and embraced his
feet, lamenting bitterly. And all his slaves and
women-slaves came and stood around his couch,
greatly lamenting Then came Abraham into indifference of death,[2] and Death said to Abraham :
Come, embrace my right hand, and let cheerfulness
and life and strength come to thee. For Death
deceived Abraham , and he embraced his hand,
and straightway his soul clave to the hand of Death.
And straightway Michael the archangel stood by
him with a host of angels, and they raised his
precious soul in their hands in a cloth divinely
woven,[3] and they tended the body of the just Abraham with exquisite ointments and perfumes until
the third day after his death ;[4] and they buried him

[1] Note the anachronism—Sarah is still alive
[2] Gk εἰς ὀλιγωρίαν θανάτου
[3] So in Christian art angels are represented as carrying souls
in a linen cloth (James)
[4] *until the third day after his death* There are occasional
traces in Jewish literature of the belief that the soul hovers in
the neighbourhood of the body during the three days immediately
following death , after which it departs to adore God and then
enters Paradise cf *Test Job*, end (" after three days Job saw
the angels come for his soul "), cf also *Apocalypse of Zephaniah*
(as cited by Bousset, *R J*[2], p 341). In the Ezra-Apocalypse

in the promised land, by the oak of Mamre; [1] but
the angels escorted his precious soul, and ascended
into heaven singing the hymn of the " Thrice-holy " [2]
to the Lord God of all; and they set it to adore [3]
the God and Father   And after much praising and
glorifying unto the Lord, and when Abraham had
adored, there came the pure voice of the God and
Father, saying thus   Uplift, then, my friend
Abraham into Paradise, where are the tabernacles
of my righteous ones, and the abodes [4] of my holy
ones, Isaac and Jacob, in his bosom, [5] where is no
toil, neither grief nor mourning; but peace and

(cf 4 Ezra vii 101) it is said that the (righteous) soul enjoys
seven days' freedom before entering into its " habitation ",
before this consummation is reached it " adores " the Most
High, cf 4 Ezra vii 78   The seven days' freedom is also
attested in the Talmud (*T   B   Shabb*, 152 *a* and *b*   See
E A, p 153, cf also *Vita Adæ et Evæ*   Charles, *op cit*, p 144
Cf also the *Apocalypse of Paul*, § 17 (James, *Ap N T*, p 534)
a soul appears before God weeping and saying   " *Have mercy on
me   for to-day it is seven days since I went forth out of my
body,*" etc
    [1] According to Genesis xxv 7–9 Abraham was buried beside
Sarah in the care of Machpelah by Isaac and Ishmael
    [2] The recital of the Trisagion is a part of the angelic worship
cf Isaiah vi, and Ezek iii, and see Abrahams, *Annotated Jewish
Prayer Book*, p xlvi   In 1 Enoch xxxix 12 the Trisagion is the
song of the angelic watchers
    [3] Cf 4 Ezra vii 78
    [4] Or " Mansions " (Gk μοναί   cf John xiv 2)
    [5] Apparently " to sit in Abraham's lap or bosom " meant to
enjoy the bliss of Paradise, cf Luke xvi 23   An exact parallel
to the phrase occurs in the Talmud (*T B Kidd*, 72 *b*), where it
is said of a certain third-century Babylonian Rabbi (Adda bar
Ahaba), that he " sits in the bosom of Abraham," *i e* probably at his death he entered into Paradise.   For the supposed
parallel in 4 Macc xiii 16–17 see the interesting note of Dr I
Abrahams, *Studies*, 2nd series, p 202 f, and James, *Testament*,
pp 72 ff   For the confusion in the text (Isaac and Jacob " in his
bosom ") see p xxvi.

exultation, and life everlasting.   [1] [*Let us, too, my
beloved brethren, imitate the hospitality of the patriarch
Abraham, and let us gain his virtuous behaviour, that
we may be counted worthy of eternal life, glorifying the
Father, Son and Holy Spirit : His be the glory and
the power for ever.   Amen*] [1]

[1-1] The doxology appears to be a Christian addition.

PART II · THE SHORTER RECENSION
(14 chapters)

Michael's commission. (Chapter I.)

I. IT came to pass when the days of Abraham's death drew nigh, that the Lord said unto Michael : Arise, go to Abraham my servant, and say unto him : Thou shalt depart from life, for, lo ! the years of thy temporal life are fulfilled that he may set the affairs of his household in order ere he die.

The Archangel visits Abraham, and at last the object of his mission is disclosed. (Chapters II-VII)

II. So Michael went and came to Abraham and found him sitting before his oxen for ploughing, and he was exceeding aged in form, and he was holding his son in his arms.[1] So Abraham saw the archangel Michael, and arose from the ground and saluted him, not witting who it was and said unto him . May God keep thee safe ! Mayest thou continue on thy journey prosperously.[2] And Michael

---

[1] This curious detail—which can hardly be original—is peculiar to Rec B, it is omitted in some important texts (A and C) Isaac, of course, appears elsewhere in the narrative as a grown-up man

[2] *Mayest thou continue thy journey prosperously ·* Gk. ἄναστα καλῶς πορευόμενος τὴν ὁδόν σου

answered him · Thou art kind, noble father   And
Abraham answered and said unto him   Come,
draw nigh unto me, brother, and sit thou down a
short season, that I may order a beast to be brought,
that we may depart unto my house, and that thou
mayest abide with me, for it is nigh unto eventide.
Early in the morning rise up and go whithersoever
thou listest, lest any evil beast meet thee and wound
thee   And Michael enquired of Abraham and said :
Tell me thy name before I enter thy house, lest I be
burdensome unto thee.   Abraham answered and
said   My parents named me Abram, and the Lord
gave me a new name, Abraham,[1] saying.   *Arise, and
journey from thy house and from thy kindred, even
hither into a land which I shall show you* [2]   And when
I had departed into the land which the Lord showed
me, he said unto me, *Thy name shall no more be called
Abram, but thy name shall be Abraham* [1]   Michael
answered and said unto him · Pardon me, my father,
man that hast been cared for by God, for I am a
stranger, and I heard concerning thee when thou
didst depart a space of forty furlongs, and didst
take a calf, and offer it, entertaining angels in thy
house that they might rest [3]   Thus conversing the
two of them arose, and went within the house.
Then Abraham called one of his servants and said
to him   Go, bring me a beast of burden that the
stranger may sit thereon, for he is weary from his

[1] Cf Gen xvii. 5
[2] Cf Gen xii 1
[3] Cf Gen xviii   The detail about Abraham going a distance
of forty furlongs to secure a calf is an embellishment of the
Biblical narrative · cf Gen xviii 7

journey. And Michael said . Trouble not the boy, but let us go walking until we come unto thy house, for I love thy companionship

III. They arose and began to go, and as they drew near to the city, about three furlongs away, they found a mighty fruit-tree having three hundred branches like unto a tamarisk.[1] And they heard a voice singing from its branches · Holy art thou, for thou hast kept the purpose concerning those things for which thou wast sent. And Abraham heard the voice and hid the mystery in his heart, saying to himself . What, then, is the mystery which I have heard? And as they came within the house Abraham said to his servants · Arise, go out to the flocks, and bring three lambs, and slay them quickly, and serve them, that we may eat and drink; for this day is a day of good cheer. And the servants brought the sheep, and Abraham called his son Isaac, and said unto him   Son Isaac, rise up, and put water in the bason that we may wash the feet of this stranger   And he brought it as he was bidden. Then said Abraham . I have a feeling of what shall even come to pass, that in this bowl I shall never again wash the feet of a stranger entertained by us   And when Isaac heard his father speaking these words, he wept and said unto him :

---

[1] *having three hundred branches like unto a tamarisk*. This feature is original—Rec A makes the tree a cypress   The numerical value of the letters of the Hebrew word for *tamarisk tree* (אשׁל) = 331, which is no doubt the correct number for the branches in the text   Abraham planted a tamarisk tree at Beersheba (Gen xxi 33)   Sacred trees are often mentioned in the early stages of religion. For a tree-oracle cf. 2 Sam v 24

My father, what is this that thou saidst, 'Tis the last time for me to wash a stranger's feet? And Abraham saw his son weeping, and he himself wept too exceedingly; and Michael saw them weeping, and he also wept, and the tears of Michael fell upon the bason and became a precious stone [1]

IV. Now when Sarah heard their lamenting, she being within in her house, came out and spake to Abraham : Why is it that ye weep thus, my lord? Abraham answered and said unto her · 'Tis nought evil, go in into thy abode and do thine own business lest we become troublesome to the stranger. So Sarah went in, as she was minded to make ready the supper. And the sun approached the setting, and Michael went out from the house and was caught up into the heavens to worship in the presence of God, for at sunset all angels worship God,[2] and the same Michael is first of the angels. And all worshipped and departed, each unto his place. But Michael answered in the presence of God and said : Lord, bid me be questioned in the presence of thy

[1] Rec A has the plural (" precious stones ")

[2] Michael has to lead the hymn of praise sung by the choir of ministering angels in heaven, which happens every day (after sunset) As this time has now arrived (it is now past sunset) the archangel absents himself for a short time and ascends to heaven   For the representation cf Yalkut § 133 (on Gen xxxii 25 ff), where Michael, who is wrestling with Jacob, asks to be released (ver 27) that he may lead the heavenly choir   " Every day the Holy One creates new angels and they sing a hymn before Him and depart " (T B Hag , 14 a)   See also Pirke d. R Eliezer (ed Friedlander), Chap IV , cf also Bereshith rabba, § 78 (on Gen xxxii 26)   According to T B Hag , 12b, the ministering angels utter the song in the night (thus not interfering with Israel's praise during the day), and are silent by day   See further Lueken, Michael, p 39

holy glory. And the Lord said to Michael: Tell what thou desirest. The archangel answered and said : Lord, thou didst send me to Abraham to say unto him : Depart thou from out of thy body, and go thou from the world. The Lord doth call thee. And I do not dare, Lord, to show myself to him, for he is thy friend and a righteous man making strangers welcome. But I beseech thee, Lord, bid the remembrance of Abraham's death to enter into his own heart, and let me not tell it to him. For 'tis great abruptness to say : Depart from the world; and above all from his own body. For thou didst from the beginning make him to pity all men's souls. Then said the Lord unto Michael: Arise, go to Abraham, and sojourn with him, and whatever thou seest him eating, eat thou too; and wherever he resteth, rest thou there too. For I will inject the notion [1] of Abraham's death into the heart of Isaac his son in a dream

V. Then Michael went away to the house of Abraham in that evening and found them making ready the supper, and they ate and drank and made merry. And Abraham said to his son Isaac : Arise, son, and spread the couch of the stranger that he may rest, and put the lamp upon the lamp-stand. And Isaac did as his father bade. And Isaac said to his father . Father, I, too, am coming to sleep beside you. Abraham answered him : Not so, my son, lest we be burdensome to this stranger, but depart, and rest in thine own chamber. And Isaac,

---

[1] *I will inject the notion.* Gk ἐγὼ γὰρ ῥίψω τὴν μνήμην.

not wishing to disobey his father's command, departed to rest in his own chamber.

VI Now it came to pass about the seventh hour of the night Isaac [1] awoke from sleep, and came to the door of his father's abode, knocking and saying: Father, open, that I may enjoy the sight of thee [2] before they take thee away from me   And Abraham rose and opened and Isaac entered and hung upon the neck of his father, weeping, and in lamentation he began to kiss him, and Abraham wept with his son   And Michael saw them weeping, and he himself wept too, and Sarah heard the lamentation from her bed-chamber, and knocked, saying My Lord Abraham, why this lamentation?   Has the stranger told thee concerning thy nephew Lot, that he has died?   Or hath aught else happened unto us?   And Michael answered and said unto Sarah   Not so, Sarah, I brought no word concerning Lot   But I knew concerning all your kindness, that ye excel all the men on the earth, and God remembered you   Then said Sarah to Abraham How didst thou dare to weep when the man of God came in unto thee?   And why did thine eyes weep for the man? [3]   For to-day there is gladness. So Abraham said unto her   Whence knowest thou that he is a man of God?   And Sarah answered and

---

[1] i e immediately after midnight, the time most congenial for the reception of divine revelation   Cf *T B Berak* 3*b* (David rose at midnight to study Torah)   According to Rec A (Chap V) Isaac rose " at the third hour of the night "—here again Rec B is more original

[2] Gk ἀπολαύσω

[3] Gk πῶς ἐδάκρυσάν σου οἱ ὀφθαλμοὶ τῶν ζευμάτων τοῦ φωτός, i e " why wept the eyes of the fountain of light? "

said . Because I declare and tell thee that this is one of the three men who sojourned with us at the oak of Mamre, when one of the slaves went and brought a calf and thou didst sacrifice it. And thou saidst unto me   Arise, prepare that we may eat with these men in our house. And Abraham answered and said   Thou hast bethought thee well, my wife, for I too when I washed his feet knew in my heart that these were the feet which I did wash at the oak of Mamre; and as I began to enquire of his journey, he said   I go to guard thy kinsman Lot from Sodom; [1] and then I recognized the mystery.

VII. Then Abraham said to Michael : Tell me, man of God, and reveal unto me why thou art come hither   Michael said . Thy son Isaac will declare unto thee.   Abraham said to his son : My beloved son, tell me what thou didst see in a dream to-day, and what thou wast told.   Tell me   Isaac answered his father   I saw in a dream the sun and the moon   And a crown was upon my head, and there was a man of gigantic size shining mightily from heaven,[2] as the light that is called father of the light.[3]   And he took the sun from my head, but left behind its rays with me.   And I wept and said · I beseech

[1] Thus according to Rec B Michael, on the occasion described in Gen xviii 1–10, departed to rescue Lot (cf *Bereshith rabba*, § 12), whereas according to Rec A he remained as chief speaker of the three

[2] *a man of gigantic size*, etc   Michael is here depicted as the cosmic man   cf Dan vii 13

[3] *father of the light*   The phrase " the light of the universe, the father of light," occurs in *Apoc Moses*, § xlvi   There the divine (uncreated) light is referred to (not apparently the light of the sun), cf James, 1 17   Here Michael appears to be invested with this divine light.

thee, my lord, do not carry off the glory from my head, and the light of my house, and all my glory. And the sun and the moon and the stars wept, saying : Do not carry off the glory of our might And that radiant man answered and said unto me : Weep not because I take the light of thy house, for it is taken away from toils into rest, from lowliness into exaltation, they raise him from confinement into spaciousness; they raise him from darkness into light. I said unto him · I beseech thee, Lord, take also the rays with him   He said to me : Twelve hours of the day there are,[1] and then I will take all the rays   As the radiant man said these words I saw the sun and my house ascending into heaven, but that crown saw I no more. And that sun was like thee, my father. And Michael said to Abraham : Thy son Isaac has spoken truth.   For thou shalt go, and be taken up into the heavens, but thy body shall remain upon the earth until seven thousand ages are fulfilled.[2] For then shall all flesh be raised. So now, Abraham, settle the affairs of thine household, and take order concerning thy children, for fully hast thou heard thy apportioned fate. Then Abraham answered and said unto Michael : I beseech thee, Lord, if I must needs leave my body, I would fain be caught up in the body, that I may see the creatures which the Lord my God has created in heaven and upon earth. Michael answered and said : This is not my appointed

---

[1] Cf John xi 9   For the symbolic use of " twelve hours " cf *Ap Abr* pp. 76 f.

[2] *i e.* the seven thousand years which span the existence of the world, see note p 33 above, and on *Ap Abr.* xxviii.

work, but I will depart and tell the Lord concerning this, and if I am bidden I will show thee all these works.

Abraham ascends on a cloud, accompanied by the Archangel, and is shown the secrets of the other world. (Chapters VIII–XII)

VIII. Then Michael went up into the heavens, and spoke concerning Abraham in the presence of the Lord. And the Lord answered Michael: Depart, and take up Abraham in the body, and show him all, and whatsoever he sayeth unto thee, do thou for him as he is my friend So Michael went out, and caught up Abraham in the body upon a cloud, and bore him up to the river Ocean.[1] And [2] Abraham looked and saw two gates, one small, and the other great And between the two gates sat a man upon a seat of great glory. And a host of angels surrounded him. He was weeping, and, again, laughing, and his lamentation exceeded his laughter sevenfold. And Abraham said to Michael: Who is this, that sitteth between the two gates with great glory? At one time he laugheth, and anon weepeth And the lamentation exceedeth the laughter seven-fold? Then Michael said unto Abraham: Dost thou not know who he is? And he said: No, Lord. And Michael said unto Abra-

[1] i e. the Great Sea above the firmament, which according to *Test xii Patriarchs*, Levi, 2, lies between the first and second heavens cf 2 Enoch iii. 3.

[2] Here begins a section (continuing to the end of VIII) which is misplaced (cf. pp xiii f) In Rec A it correctly follows the sections describing Paradise and the place of judgement. It should follow § XII

ham · Seest thou these two gates, the small and the great? These are they which lead to life and to destruction. And this man who sits between them, this is Adam, the first man whom the Lord created. And He set him in this place to behold every soul that leaves the body; for all are sprung from him. So whenever thou beholdest him weeping, know that he has seen many souls being led away into destruction; but whenever thou seest him laughing, he has seen a few souls being led away into life. Seest thou how the lamentation exceeds the laughter? Because he beholds the most part of the world being led away through the broad gate into destruction, therefore his lamentation exceeds his laughter sevenfold.

IX. Abraham said   He who cannot enter through the strait gate, can he not enter into life? Then Abraham wept saying · Woe is me! what shall I do? I am a man broad in body, and how shall I be able to enter into the strait gate, by which a child of fifteen years cannot enter? Michael answered and said unto Abraham · Fear thou not, father, neither be grieved, for thou shalt enter through it without hindrance, thou and all like unto thee. Now while Abraham stood and marvelled, lo, an angel of the Lord driving sixty thousand souls of sinners to destruction. And Abraham said unto Michael · Are all these going to destruction? And Michael said unto him: Yea, but let us go and search among these souls, to see if there be even one of them righteous   And as they went, they found an angel holding in his hand one soul of a woman from among the sixty thousand, because he found her sins equally balanced with all her works; and they were neither in motion nor at rest, but in a condition midway between them; but those other souls they carried into destruction. And Abraham said unto Michael . Lord, is this the angel that removes the souls from the body, or not? Michael answered and said : This is Death, and he leads them away into the place of the judgement, that the judge may judge them.

X. And Abraham said : My Lord, I beseech thee that thou bring me up into the place of judgement that I too may see how they are judged. Then Michael took Abraham upon a cloud and brought him into Paradise. And when he reached the place where was the judge, the angel came and gave that soul to the judge And the soul said · Have mercy on me, Lord, Lord And the judge said · How shall I have mercy on thee when thou hadst no mercy on thy daughter which thou didst bear, the fruit of thy womb? Why didst thou slay her? And it answered : Nay, Lord, the murder came not from me, but my daughter herself lied against me. So the judge bade come him who wrote the records. And behold, cherubim holding two books; and there was with them a man exceeding great in stature. And he had upon his head three crowns, and the one crown was higher than the other two crowns And the crowns are called crowns of witness; and the man held in his hand a golden pen. The judge said to him : Show forth the sin of this soul And that man opened one of the books

F

that belonged unto the cherubim, and sought out the sin of the woman's soul, and found it. And the judge said . O wretched soul, how sayest thou that thou didst not do murder? Didst thou not go after thy husband's death, and commit adultery with thy daughter's husband, and slay her? And he convicted her also of her other sins, all that she had done from her youth. When the woman heard these things, she cried out, saying : Woe, woe is me ! because all the sins which I did in the world I forgot : but here they were not forgotten ! Then they carried her away, and delivered her to the tormentors.

XI. And Abraham said to Michael : Lord, who is this judge, and who is the other, who convicts the sins ? And Michael said to Abraham : Dost thou see the judge ? This is Abel, who first testified,[1] and God brought him hither to judge. And he who bears witness here is the teacher of heaven and earth, and the scribe of righteousness, Enoch.[2] For the Lord sent them hither to record the sins and righteousnesses of each. Abraham said : How is Enoch able to bear the weight of the souls, not having seen death ? Or, how can he give sentence to all the souls ? Michael said : If he give sentence concerning the souls it is not accepted. But it is not Enoch's business to give sentence, but it is

---

[1] *Abel, who first testified.* Gk ὁ Ἄβελ ὁ ἐν πρώτοις μαρτυρήσας Abel was the first martyr.

[2] Enoch acts as permanent recorder and scribe of righteousness   For the representation of Enoch as a *teacher*, cf *Jubilees*, iv 17   and as scribe cf 1 Enoch xii 3-4, 2 Enoch xxiii 1-3, Targ Ps Jonathan on Gen v 24 (" his name was called Metatron, the Great Scribe ").

the Lord who gives sentence, and his (Enoch's) task is only to write. For Enoch prayed the Lord saying : Lord I am fain not to give sentence to the souls, lest I become grievous to any And the Lord said to Enoch : I will bid thee to record the sins of a soul that makes atonement, and it shall enter into life. As for the soul that makes not atonement and repents, thou shalt find its sins recorded, and it shall be cast into punishment.

XII. And after Abraham had beheld the place of judgement,[1] the cloud carried him down to the firmament beneath. And Abraham looked down upon the earth,[2] and saw a man committing adultery with a married woman. And Abraham turned and said to Michael : Dost thou behold this sin? But, Lord, send fire from heaven that it may devour them. And immediately fire descended and devoured them, for the Lord had said to Michael Whatsoever Abraham shall ask thee to do for him, do thou. And again Abraham looked and saw other men slandering their companions, and he said : Let the earth open and swallow them up. And

[1] According to Rec A (Chap XI) Michael directed the heavenly chariot eastward, and showed Abraham the heavenly Paradise This, according to 2 Enoch xlii 3, " is open to the third heaven " (cf also 2 Enoch viii–x) The " place of judgement " is represented as near at hand in the same region, in fact the judgement takes place at the gates of Paradise For the idea of wickedness in heaven, cf. Ephes vi 12 (" the spiritual hosts of wickedness in the heavens "), and see further Charles's note on 2 Enoch x 1 According to *Yalḳut* on *Eccles* § 976, Gehenna is separated from Paradise by only a hand breadth (a dictum of R Hanina). Ultimately Satan was cast out of heaven with his angels (cf. Rev xii 7 ff)

[2] In the third heaven, Abraham would be above the firmament Cf *Ap Abr* xix, where Abraham from the seventh heaven surveys the various heavens and the earth, which are below him

while he yet spake, the earth swallowed them up alive. And again the cloud brought him to another place, and Abraham saw certain men going into a desert place to commit murder; and he said unto Michael   Dost thou behold this wickedness? But let wild beasts come out from the desert and tear them in pieces   And in that very hour there came forth wild beasts from the desert, and devoured them. Then the Lord God spake unto Michael saying . Turn Abraham away unto his house, and let him not go round all the creation which I have made; for he has no mercy upon sinners, but I have mercy on sinners, so that they turn again and live and repent of their sins, and be saved. And about the ninth hour Michael turned Abraham back to his own house.   And Sarah his wife, because she had not seen what had become of Abraham, was consumed with grief and gave up her soul. And after his return Abraham found her dead, and buried her

The Angel of Death visits Abraham.
(Chapter XIII)

XIII Now when the days of the death of Abraham drew nigh the Lord God spake unto Michael : Death will not dare to draw nigh to carry away the soul of my servant, because he is my friend; but do thou depart and deck out Death with great beauty, and so send him to Abraham that he may behold him with his eyes. Then Michael straightway, as he was bidden, decked out Death with great beauty, and so sent him to Abraham, that he might behold him. And he sat him down nigh unto Abraham, and when Abraham saw Death seated nigh unto him he was afraid with exceeding great fear And Death said to Abraham · Hail, holy soul · hail, dear friend of the Lord God; hail, consolation and entertainment of wayfarers. And Abraham said : Thou art welcome, servant of the Most High God. I beseech thee, tell me who thou art, and enter into my house, and partake of meat and drink, and depart from me. For since I saw thee seated nigh unto me, my soul has been disquieted. For I am altogether unworthy to come nigh unto thee, for thou art a most high spirit, but I am flesh and blood, and therefore I cannot endure thy glory. For I behold thy beauty that it is not of this world. Then Death said to Abraham : I say unto thee, in all the creation which God has made there has not been found one like unto thee, for even God Himself by searching has not found such an one on all the earth And Abraham said · How hast thou dared to lie ? For I see thy beauty that it is not of this world. And Death said unto Abraham · Think not, Abraham, that this is my beauty or that even thus I come to every man. But if a man is righteous as thou art, I take garlands then, and come to him; but if he is a sinner I come in great corruption and from their sin I make a crown for my head and trouble them with great fear, insomuch that they are dismayed So Abraham said unto him Whence comes this beauty ? Death said . There is no other more full of corruption than

I. Abraham said to him : Art thou he that is called Death ? He answered him, and said : I am the bitter name.[1] I am lamentation. . . .

Death discloses his terrors to Abraham. The death and burial of the Patriarch. (Chapter XIV)

XIV. And Abraham said to Death : Show us thy corruption   And Death revealed his corruption ; and he had two heads : the one head had the face of a serpent, and by it some meet their end suddenly through vipers ; and the other head was like a sword ; and so some meet their end by the sword, as by arrows

In that day the servants of Abraham met their end through fear of Death ; and when Abraham saw them he prayed to the Lord, and He raised them up. Then God returned and drew out the soul of Abraham as in a dream, and the archangel Michael took it up into heaven.

And Isaac buried his father beside his mother Sarah, glorifying and praising God : for to Him is due glory, honour, and worship, of the Father, Son, and Holy Spirit, now and ever, world without end.   Amen.

---

[1] An allusion to the meaning of the name of the Angel of Death (*Sammael* = ? " venom of God ").

APPENDIX

By S. GASELEE, M.A.

INTRODUCTORY NOTE

THE Coptic version of the Testaments of Abraham, Isaac, and Jacob is found in the Vatican Coptic Manuscript No 61, ff. 163b–189b, and has been printed by I. Guidi, *Rendiconti della Reale Accademia dei Lincei, Classe di scienze morali, Storiche, e Pilologiche, Serie Quinta, Vol. IX* (Rome, 1900), pp 157–180, 223–264. A German translation of the two latter was made by E Andersson, *Sphinx, Vol VII* (Upsala, 1903), pp 77–94, 129–142.

The manuscript bears the date A D. 962, which is comparatively early for the Northern or Bohairic dialect in which these texts are found Andersson calls attention to a few undoubted Sa'idicisms, or traces of the Southern dialect, and it is quite likely that the Testaments, which in the Coptic form part of sermons or homiletical discourses, were put from Sa'idic into Bohairic as the latter became more and more the ecclesiastical dialect of the whole of Lower Egypt.

Andersson's translation is accurate and reliable, except for two grammatical points, too technical for discussion here, in his notes 14 and 17 to the *Testament of Isaac*, which I have corrected in the

English version here given, I have consulted his work throughout, and differ from him, when I do so, after consideration and with respect   I have tried to preserve in my translation as much of the " feeling " of the Coptic language as is compatible with intelligible English, the reader will perhaps note the constant *asyndeton* which is so characteristic of idiomatic Coptic.

There are some obvious dislocations or gaps in the Coptic texts.   In the *Testament of Isaac*, for instance, after the words " a virgin called Mary " (f. 169*a*), the subject suddenly changes back from our Lord to the Patriarch, and at the end of f 169*a* and the beginning of f. 169*b* there is an allusion to Isaac's recovery of his sight, though there has been no previous mention of his blindness; and later on the same page " the priest of God " is introduced without any explanation as to who the priest was   The sudden change from third person to first on f 172*b* may have been in the original story, though this seems less likely in a similar change in the *Testament of Jacob* (f. 184*a*)   On the whole, however, the texts are in good condition, and the violent treatment to which the *Testaments* (more especially the *Testament of Jacob*) have been subjected, lies a long way behind their present Coptic form.

I. THE TESTAMENT OF ISAAC
(Cod Copt. Vat. 61, f. 164a.)

THIS is the coming forth from the body (σωμα) of the Patriarch (πατριαρχης) Isaac, the son of Abraham, on the twenty-eighth day of the month Mesore,[1] in the peace (εἰρηνη) of God   Amen.

Now (δε) the Patriarch (πατριαρχης) Isaac wrote his Testament (διαθηκη) and spake his words for the instruction of Jacob his son and of all them that were gathered together unto him, so that the blessings of the Patriarch (πατριαρχης) should be upon those that heard, and upon those also that should come after them

Hearken unto these words of instruction and these refreshing medicines, so that the will of God may be done always upon him that hearkeneth, not only with the outward ear, but (ἀλλα) in the depth of the heart, and remaineth in faith without doubting: even as (κατα-) it is written: If thou hear a word, let it remain with thee, (f 164b) that is, that a man should strive (ἀγωνιζεσθαι), when he hath heard it, with endurance (ὑπομονη), and God shall give him a blessing in that after which he hath sought. And again it is written: He shall deny them nothing which the sons of men have asked (αἰτειν) upon

[1] September 4   Commemoration of the Patriarchs Abraham, Isaac, and Jacob in the Coptic calendar

the earth. For (γαρ) if God hath given power (ἐξουσια) to us over every thing that is upon the earth, how much more (ποσῳ μαλλον) to him who shall be established in his faith in the words of God and of His saints, not in unbelief (-ἀπιστος), but (ἀλλα) in a heart made straight in the words of God and of all His saints : and he shall be made an inheritor (κληρονομος) with the saints in the kingdom of God   But God is compassionate and merciful, who hath accepted robbers and publicans (τελωνης) in the generations (γενεα) that are gone by, because of their innocence (ἀκεραιος) and their faith that was righteous and (f. 165a) surely founded in God   and likewise shall He be with all the generations (γενεα) that are to come

Now it came to pass that when the days of our father the patriarch (πατριαρχης) Isaac were come nigh that he should come forth from the body (σωμα), God the merciful sent unto him the great holy archangel (ἀρχαγγελος) Michael, the same that He had sent unto Abraham his father.   At the hour of dawn on the twenty-second day of Mesore he said unto him : Hail (χαιρε), my son, the chosen of God, and His beloved son : now as for the God-loving and righteous (δικαιος) old man, our father Isaac, it was his custom (συνηθεια) daily to speak with the holy angels   He cast down his face, he saw him, that he was in the likeness of his father Abraham ; he opened his mouth, he lifted up his voice, he cried out in great joy and exultation   I am looking upon thy face even as one that hath looked upon God. The   angel (ἀγγελος) said : Take thought, my

beloved Isaac (f. 165b), for I have been sent for thee
from the living God, to take thee to the heavens
unto thy father Abraham, and that thou mayest
keep festival with all the saints, for (γαρ) thy
father Abraham keepeth watch over thee, and
cometh for thee himself But (πλην) behold thy
throne (θρονος), it is set up for thee in the heavens,
near unto thy father Abraham. As for thee and thy
beloved son Jacob, ye shall be with an high inheritance (κληρος) that belongeth to all that are in the
kingdom of the heavens, in the glory of the Father,
and the Son, and the Holy Ghost (πνευμα), for they
shall call you by this name unto all generations
(γενεα), namely, Patriarch (πατριαρχης) and father
of all the earth (κοσμος) But the God-loving old
man our father Isaac answered and said unto the
angel (αγγελος) I am astonished at thee exceedingly Art thou not (μη) my father Abraham?
The angel (αγγελος) said My beloved Isaac, I am
the angel that ministers (διακονειν) unto thy
(f. 166a) father Abraham Now indeed rejoice
and be glad, and be not troubled, for thou shalt
not be taken in pain, but it is a rejoicing that thou
shalt be taken in honour and rest for ever Thou
shalt be taken from a prison unto a broad place
Thou shalt be taken unto joy unfailing, and gladness,
and light, and pleasure (ευφροσυνη), and rejoicing,
and unfailing freshness But (λοιπον) set in order
thy testament (διαθηκη) and the instruction of thy
house, so that thou mayest be translated unto rest :
after that, blessed is thy father that begat thee,
and blessed art thou thyself : blessed is thy son

Jacob, blessed is thy seed (σπερμα) that cometh after thee.

Now (δε) Jacob heard them talking one with the other : he came, he gave ear unto them, but spake not. Our father Isaac said unto the angel (ἀγγελος) with pity in his heart · (f 166b) What shall I do with the light of mine eyes, Jacob, my beloved son ? I am afraid because of Esau : thou knowest thyself all the matter. The angel (ἀγγελος) said unto him : O my beloved Isaac, if all the Gentiles (ἐθνος) that are in the earth (κοσμος) were gathered together into one place, they would not be able to loosen the blessing thou hast spoken over Jacob in the hour when thou didst bless him The Father hath blessed him : Michael, and all the angels, and all the heavenly ones, and the spirits (πνευμα) of all the righteous (δικαιος), and thy father Abraham, all have answered Amen The steel shall not come nigh him, but (ἀλλα) he shall be exalted exceedingly and shall spread abroad , he shall be made a mighty nation (ἐθνος), and twelve tribes (φυλη) shall come forth from him Our father Isaac said unto the angel (ἀγγελος) : Thou hast comforted me exceedingly But (ἀλλα) let not Jacob know, so that he may not be troubled and weep, because (f. 167a) never have I given him pain The angel (ἀγγελος) of the Lord said unto him . O my beloved Isaac, blessed is every righteous (δικαιος) man that cometh forth from the body · blessed are they in their meeting (ἀπανταν) with God Woe, woe, woe unto three times to the sinner, because he has been born into the world (κοσμος) Trouble must

there be, O my beloved · therefore do thou thyself
instruct thy sons after thy way and all the things
which thy father did command thee   Hide nothing
from Jacob, so that (ἵνα) he may write them down
unto all the generations (γενεα) that come after
him, that all they that love God may work according
to them, and obtain for themselves everlasting life.
But (ἀλλα) do thou by all means (παντως) take
thought,[1] because I come unto thee in joy, without
delay.   The peace (εἰρηνη) which the Lord gave
unto us, I give it unto thee · for I must depart with
all speed unto Him that sent me

Now (δε) when the angel (ἀγγελος) had said this,
he arose above the bed (f. 167b) of our father Isaac;
he departed (ἀναχωρειν) while our father Isaac
watched after him   And he was astonished at the
revelation which he had seen, and he said : I shall
not see the light until I shall be sought   Now (δε)
while he was saying this, behold Jacob arose : he
came nigh unto the door of the bed-chamber (κοιτων)
of his father : now the angel (ἀγγελος) had cast a
slumber upon him, so that he should not hear them
speaking   And (δε) when he had come nigh unto
the place wherein his father slept, he said unto him :
My father, with whom speakest thou ?   His father
said : Unto Isaac : Dost thou hear me, O my son ?
Thine aged father hath been sent for to be taken
from thee, O my beloved son.   He cast his arms
about his father , he wept, saying unto him · My
strength hath gone and hath left me; thou hast

[1] The meaning here, as of the same expression in f 165a *fin.*,
is something between " meditate " and " set thy affairs in order "

made me an orphan (ὀρφανος), O my father;
(f. 168a) I am become fatherless and wretched
to-day. And our father Isaac cast his arms about
Jacob; he kissed him; both wept until they ceased,
while Jacob said . take me with thee, O my beloved
Isaac, my blessed father But his father said:
I cannot so ordain, my beloved Jacob But (ἀλλα)
thanks be unto God that thou too art a father, O
my beloved. Tarry until thou art sent for   I also
remember a day when the high and flourishing
(φορειν) cypress (κυπαρισσος) was moved, while I
spake unto my lord and father Abraham, and I
could do nothing. So now, O my son, the ordinance
which God hath ordained for each one according to His
power—it is come to pass, for the things which are
written may not be altered. But (πλην) the Lord
knoweth, my son, that behold my heart is heavy
indeed because of thee : beside this (παλιν) I
rejoice in my going unto the Lord So now make
thyself strong in a prince-(f. 168b)-ly (ἡγεμονικος)
spirit, (πνευμα), and be silent from weeping thus
with exceeding weeping   Hearken unto me, O my
beloved son, that I may speak with thee.   Where
is the first creation (πρωτοπλασμα) that God made
with His own hands, I mean our father Adam and
our mother Eve (Ζωη) ? where are Abel, and Seth ?
where are Enos and Mahalaleel ? where are Jared
and my father Enoch ? where are Methuselah and
Lamech ? where is our father Noah, and his three
sons, Shem, Ham, Japheth ? After these Arphaxad
and Cainan and Salah and Eber and Reu and Serug
and Nahor and Terah, and my father Abraham and

Lot his brother : and all these tasted (-πειρα) of
death (f. 169a) saving only our father Enoch the
perfect (τελειος), who was taken up unto the
heavenly parts (ἐπουρανιος) of the skies. After
these, therefore (οὖν), there are twelve generations
(γενεα) that shall come from thee, so that Jesus Christ
may come forth from thy seed (σπερμα), from a
virgin (παρθενος) called Mary.

And God was with him until he had completed
an hundred years, and he did fast (νηστευειν) every
day until sunset, offering up his sacrifices (θυσια),
and those of his household, for the salvation of his
soul (ψυχη), and passing the half of the day in his
ascetic practices (ἀσκησις) and the half of the night
praying unto God : and so he did unto many years
And thrice in (κατα) the year did he pass forty days
without eating, and he drank no wine and ate no
fruit (ὀπωρα) and slept not on a bed nor (οὐδε)
upon a mattress : and he did pray unto God.

Now (δε) when the multitude heard that the
man of God could see clearly, (f. 169b) they came
together unto him from every country (χωρα) and
from every place, to hearken unto his instructions
of life, knowing that a spirit (πνευμα) of God was
speaking in him. The great ones that were gathered
together unto him said unto him : Our holy father,
what is the ordinance that hath been delivered to
thee, after this long time on this sort since the
light of thine eyes was dimmed ? [1] lo and behold,
now thou seest clearly But (δε) he, the God-
loving old man, opened his mouth in laughter and

[1] I it " was weighed down, was heavy "

said unto them · My sons and my beloved brethren, it is God that hath healed me. When he saw that I had approached unto the gate (πυλη) of death, He caused this to happen to me as a consolation in my old age.

But (δε) the priest of God said unto him : Show me the way unto a word of consolation. He said unto him : Keep thy body (σωμα) holy, because it is the temple of God, and the spirit (πνευμα) of God dwelleth in it. (f. 170a) Keep also thy little flesh (σαρξ) pure and holy. Keep thyself, mingle not with men, so that no word of wrath may come out of thy mouth Keep thyself from slander (καταλαλια). Keep thyself from vain-glory. Keep thyself, speak not alone with a woman. Keep thyself, speak no idle (αργος) word from thy mouth. Keep thy hands, so that they be not stretched out to that which is not thine Offer not up a sacrifice (θυσια) when there is a blemish in thee Wash in water at the hour when thou desirest to come nigh the altar (θυσιαστηριον) Mingle not the thoughts of the world (κοσμος) with the thoughts of God in the hour when thou shalt stand before Him. Strive to be at peace (-ειρηνη) with all men in the hour when thou shalt offer up sacrifice (θυσια) to God. If thou shalt come to approach unto the altar (θυσιαστηριον), thou shalt repeat to thyself an hundred times a prayer unto God, (f 170b) making this confession (εξομολογησις), speaking after this fashion : God, the incomprehensible, the inscrutable, the invincible, the hallowed treasure, purify me in love (αγαπη), for I am flesh (σαρξ) and

blood, and I have taken refuge in Thee. I know
that I am unclean; Thou shalt cleanse me, O Lord,
who have come unto Thee bowed down before Thee
I know that I am unclean, Thou shalt cleanse me,
O Lord, who have come unto Thee bowed down so
that Thou mayest send upon me the fire that
consumeth created matter (ὕλη) It is Thy mercy
that taketh away mine iniquity (ἀνομια), forgive
me, sinner that I am, and forgive all Thy creation
which Thou hast made I have no contentions
like unto the beasts (θηριον); I am at peace (εἰρηνη)
with all that is made in Thy likeness (εἰκων); I
am untroubled by all the evil reasonings (λογισμος)
that have been made I am Thy son, I am Thy
servant, I am the son of Thine handmaid I am
the sinner, Thou art the forgiver, forgive me in
love (ἀγαπη) and hearken unto my prayer, that I
may stand (f 171a) at the altar (θυσιαστηριον)
and my sacrifice (θυσια) be made acceptable in Thy
sight Turn me not back because of my sin, but
(ἀλλα) take me unto Thyself like a sheep that is
gone astray. God that hast[1] been with our father
Adam, and Abel, and Noah, and our father Abraham,
even Thou shalt[2] be with me. Thou hast[1] been
with our father Jacob, even Thou shalt[2] be
with me and receive my sacrifice (θυσια) from my
hand.

When thou hast rehearsed this before thou goest
up to the altar, then (τοτε) come, offer up thy

---

[1] Lit "that hath been", "He that hath been"
[2] Strong future for imperative It would be equally correct
to translate "Be with me"

G

sacrifice (θυσια) and strive earnestly (-σπουδαζειν) to keep watch upon thyself, for here is the Spirit (πνευμα) of the Lord, so that thou shouldst not vex Him · for the work of a priest is no small work. It beseemeth every one among the priests to-day, and unto the lattermost generation (γενεα), and unto the end of the world (κοσμος), not to be filled with wine, not to be filled with bread, not to be filled with water, not to speak of the happenings (συντυχια) of this world (κοσμος), nor listen to them that speak [of them] : but (ἀλλα) they should lead all their life in-(f 171b)-stant unto prayer and watching and ascetic practice (ἀσκησις), until the Lord cometh to seek them in peace (εἰρηνη). Every man that is upon the earth, whether (εἰτε) monk (μοναχος) or (εἰτε) priest, it beseemeth them to love the well-chosen withdrawing of themselves (ἀναχωρησις) after a little time, and that they should renounce (ἀποτασσεσθαι) the world (κοσμος) and its evil cares, and remain in the holy angelic (ἀγγελικος) service in purity, and become purified before the Lord and His angels (ἀγγελος), because of their holy sacrifices (θυσια) and their angelic (ἀγγελικος) service, which is the type (τυπος) that they shall perform in the heavens. And the angels (ἀγγελος) shall be their companions because of their perfect faith and their purity, and great is their honour before God. Simply (ἀπλως), whether (εἰτε) he be small or (εἰτε) great, it is sinlessness that the Lord seeketh from him : but (δε) as for the wicked that commit sin, it behoveth them to re-(f 172a)-pent (-μετανοειν) before God Thou shalt not sin

in any of these sins : thou shalt not slay with the
sword ; thou shalt not slay with the tongue , thou
shalt not commit fornication (-πορνευειν) in thy
body (σωμα); thou shalt not commit fornication
(-πορνευειν) in thy thoughts; thou shalt not
defile thyself ; thou shalt not envy ; thou shalt
not be wroth until the sun set, nor remain in vain
glory. Thou shalt not rejoice at the fall of thine
enemy, nor (ουδε) at that of thy neighbour ; thou
shalt not blaspheme ; thou shalt not teach thy
mouth to slander (καταλαλια); thine eye shall not
look after a woman with concupiscence (επιθυμια)
Now (δε) as for these and things like unto them,
we have need (χρεια) of taking great heed, until
each one of us be saved from the wrath that shall
be revealed in heaven.

Now (δε) when the multitude that was gathered
together unto him had heard these things, they all
cried out together in a loud voice, saying : Meet
(αξιος) and (και) right (δικαιος) are these words
of truth. But (δε) the God-loving old man kept
silence : he drew up the coverlet, (f 172b) he
covered his face. Now (δε) the multitude and the
priest kept silence, while he should repose a little .
but (δε) the angel (αγγελος) of his father came unto
him ; he took him up to the heavens. And he saw
in fear and trembling multitudes parted on this
side and on that, after the fashion (τυπος) of the
last day, and it was a great consternation to see
them. Some had faces of camels, others had faces
of lions and hyænas and leopards, others had faces
of dogs, others had one eye, which was a fearful

thing in them. And (δε) I beheld, and lo one was brought being pursued, and (δε) when they came unto the beasts (θηριον), they who were going with him drew to one side : the lions came nigh unto him, they rent him in the midst, they tare him limb (μελος) from limb (μελος), they rent him, they ate him Then did they cast him up again, and he became like to himself again and when [1] he came further than the lions, they likewise did thus unto him. (f. 173a) They did simply (ἁπαξ ἁπλως) give him into each other's hands, and each one would rend him and eat him and cast him up, and he would become like to himself, yea, his own self again I said unto the angel (ἀγγελος) My Lord, how many sins then (ἀρα) hath this man committed, that all these things are done unto him ? The angel (ἀγγελος) said unto me · This man whom thou hast seen hath passed five hours being at enmity with his neighbour : he died without peace (-εἰρηνη) being made with one another. Lo and behold, he is given into the hands of five tormentors (τιμωριστης) . they pass a year tormenting (τιμωρειν) him for (κατα) each hour, in requital for the five hours which he passed being at enmity with his neighbour. The angel (ἀγγελος) spake again unto me : O my beloved Isaac, thinkest thou that there are no more save these ? Believe (πιστευειμ), O my beloved Isaac, that there are seventy thousand tormentors (-τιμωρειν). Every hour that a man shall be at

---

[1] Andersson changed this word (by an alteration of one letter in the Coptic) But the singular can be kept, though the construction is then a little disconnected

enmity with his neighbour, he must go into the
hands of these tormentors (τιμωριστης), until the
end of a year of days for (κατα) each hour, (f 173*b*)
if he have not repented (-μετανοειν) of his sins before
he came forth from the body (σωμα)   He led me
further unto a river of fire : I saw that it was in
waves, and its waves were forty cubits high, and
the noise of it was like a thunder of heaven.   I
saw a multitude of souls plunged in it nine cubits
deep, and they who were in that river were crying
out, weeping with a loud voice and great sighing;
[the river] hath not afflicted the righteous (δικαιος),
but (άλλα) it is the sinners whom it doth burn,
knowing them because of the great stink that
surroundeth them   I saw the depth of the abyss,
whose smoke (καπνος) rose exceeding high; I saw a
multitude of men that were cast down therein,
crying out, weeping each one of them with his
sighing   The angel (άγγελος) said unto me : Look
down and see these others also   And (δε) when I
had seen them he said unto me : These that are
plunged down into the cold, these are they that have
committed the iniquity (άνομια) of Sodom, and so
(και γαρ) they are tormented exceedingly   (f 174*a*)
Again I saw another depth, full of sleepless worms
and snakes, and there were men that were plunged
down into it, crying out, weeping.   Again I saw
Abtelmoluchos,[1] that is set in charge of the torments
(κολασις), and he was all fire, beating the tormentors

---

[1] *i e* Temeluchus, the name of an angel who appears in
Apocalypse of Peter and elsewhere = Greek τημελοῦχος,
" care-taking ". See James, *Apoc. N 1*, p 507 *n*

(τιμωριστης) of Hell, saying unto them : Beat them, so that they they may know that God is. Again I saw another great depth, which was all fire, and there was a multitude of men beneath it, crying out, weeping, every one with sighing The angel (ἀγγελος) said unto me . Look with thine eyes and see all the punishments (κολασις). But (δε) I said unto the angel (ἀγγελος) Mine eyes reach not far enough to see them · but (ἀλλα) I will look. How long then are these in punishments (κολασις) ? He said unto me . Until the merciful God have pity upon them.

Now (δε) after these things, the angel (ἀγγελος) took me up into the heavens. I saw my father Abraham : I worshipped him, and he greeted (-ἀσπαζεσθαι) me together with all the saints. (f 174b) All of them were gathered together they honoured me because of my father. They walked with me, they took me to the veil (καταπετασμα) of the Father . I cast myself down, I worshipped Him with my father and all the saints. We all sang a hymn (-ὑμνος) unto Him, crying out and saying : Holy, holy, holy, Lord Sabaoth; heaven and earth are full of Thy holy glory. The Lord said unto my father from the holy place . Every man that shall give the name of my beloved Isaac to his son, my blessing shall be in his house for ever. Well (καλως) hast thou come, O Abraham the faithful (πιστος) ; well has thy blessed and good root come. Now indeed all requests (αἰτημα) that thou desirest, seek after them in the name of thy beloved son Isaac, and they shall be fulfilled unto thee to-day to be a

covenant (διαθηκη) for ever My father Abraham
said . Thine is the power (ἐξουσια), O Lord the
Almighty (παντοκρατωρ) (f 175a) The Lord said
unto my father from the holy place Every man
that shall give the name of my beloved Isaac unto
his son, or write his testament (διαθηκη) and lay it
in his hand for a blessing, My blessing shall not fail
in that house for ever and ever. Or if he give to
eat to a beggar that is an-hungered on the day of the
commemoration of my beloved Isaac, it shall make
him acceptable (-χαριζεσθαι) unto you in My
kingdom. My father Abraham said . Lord God
Almighty (παντοκρατωρ), if it be impossible for him
to write his testament, let Thy mercy take hold
upon him, for Thou art merciful and compassionate.
The Lord said unto Abraham · Let him give bread
unto them that are an-hungered and the poor, and
I will give him unto you in My kingdom, and he shall
come with you unto the first hour of the thousand
years Our father Abraham said If he be poor
and cannot find bread ? The Lord said Let him
pass the night of My beloved Isaac without slumber,
and I will give him unto you as an inheritor in My
kingdom (f 175b) My father Abraham said If
he be weak (ἀσθενης) and this be impossible for him,
let Thy mercy take hold upon him in love (ἀγαπη).
The Lord said unto him · Let him offer up a little
incense in My name and on the day of the commemoration of My beloved Isaac, and I will give
him to you as a son in My kingdom. And again,
if he cannot find incense, let him busy himself about
his testament and meditate (-μελεταν) upon it on

the day of My beloved Isaac thy son but (δε)
again if he know not how to meditate (-μελεταν),
let him go and listen to it from them that meditate
(-μελεταν) Again, if he can do none of these things,
let him go within his house, and shut his door upon
him, and pray an hundred times, and I will give
him to you as a son in My kingdom. But (ἀλλα)
it is better than all these if he offer up a sacrifice
(θυσια) in the name of My beloved Isaac. And
again, every one that shall do all these things that I
have spoken, they are inheritors with them that
are (f 176a) in My kingdom Every one that shall
be careful about his life (βιος) (and they that write
his testament), or do any compassionate thing,
even unto one cup of water, or he that shall write
his testament (διαθηκη) or meditate (-μελεταν)
upon it in faith with all his heart and believe
(-πιστευειν) in all these things which I have spoken,
My power and the power of the Holy Ghost (πνευμα)
shall be with them, and shall guide them in all the
world (κοσμος), and no difference (διαφορα) shall
there be in My city (πολις), and I will give them
unto you as sons in My kingdom, and they shall
come unto the first hour of the thousand years My
peace be with you all, O My holy athletes. When He
had finished saying these things, all the heavenly
ones sang a hymn (-ὑμνος), crying out and saying
Holy, holy, holy, Lord Sabaoth, heaven and earth
are full of Thy holy glory The Father spake unto
Michael from the holy place Michael, My faithful
steward, call a (f. 176b) multitude of angels (ἀγγελοι)
with all the saints. And the Lord our God went up

on the chariot (ἅρμα) of the Cherubim, while the
Seraphim went before Him, and the angels (ἄγγελοι)
and all the saints. Now (δε) when he had spoken
these things, Jacob sped unto his father Isaac; he
kissed his lips, weeping Our father Isaac touched
him, giving him a sign with the winking of his eyes,
meaning Be silent.

Our father Abraham said unto the Lord My
Lord, remember my son Isaac also answered and
said unto the Lord My Lord, remember my son
Jacob The Lord said unto him . My power shall
be with him, and he shall be glorified in My name.
He shall rule over the land of the inheritance
(κληρονομια), and the enemy shall gain no advan-
tage over him [1] Our father Isaac said unto Jacob :
My beloved son, keep this commandment (ἐντολη)
which I give into thy hand to-day. Keep watch
over thyself exceedingly. Afflict not the likeness
(εἰκων) of God, for what thou shalt have done unto
the likeness (εἰκων) of man, thou hast done unto the
likeness (εἰκων) of God, and God shall do the same
unto thee also in the hour when thou shalt meet
(-ἀπανταν) Him. This is the beginning (ἀρχη) and
the end   (f. 177a) Now (δε) when he had said this,
the Lord took away from his body (σωμα) his soul
(ψυχη), which was white like snow. He greeted
(ἀσπαζεσθαι) it, He set it upon a chariot (ἅρμα) with
Him, He took it up to the heavens, while the Seraphim went before Him and all His holy angels. He
granted (-χαριζεσθαι) unto him the good things of
His kingdom, and all requests (αἰτημα) which our

[1] Or, possibly " shall take no profit thereby " (i e the land)

father requested (αἰτειν) from the Lord, He granted (-χαριζεσθαι) them unto him for a covenant (διαθηκη) for ever.

This is the coming forth from the body (σωμα) of our lord and father Abraham and our beloved father Isaac; Abraham indeed (μεν) on the twenty-eighth day of Mesore, and (δε) Isaac too on the same twenty-eighth day of this month Mesore, being an hundred and eighty years old, And the day when our father Abraham offered him up as a sacrifice (θυσια) to God was the eighteenth day of Emshir · the heavens and the earth were full of the sweet savour of his sacrifice (θυσια) unto the Lord But (δε) our father Isaac, like silver that is tried and made excellent and purified through fire—of this sort are all who shall be purified through our father Isaac the patriarch (πατριαρχης). (f. 177b) For (γαρ) on the day when Abraham the patriarch (πατριαρχης) his father offered him up as a sacrifice (θυσια) to God, the sweet savour of his sacrifice (θυσια) went in unto the veil (καταπετασμα) of the Almighty (πιαντοκρατωρ). Blessed is every man that shall do an act of mercy on the day of the holy patriarchs (πατριαρχης) Abraham and our father Isaac, they shall be made sons unto them in the kingdom of God For our Lord hath founded a covenant (διαθηκη) with them for ever; He shall keep it with them and those that shall come after them, saying unto them Every man that shall do an act of mercy in the name of My beloved Isaac, I will give him unto you as a son in the kingdom of the heavens, and he shall come with you unto the first hour of the thousand years. So

that they shall keep festival in the ages (αἰών) of
light in the kingdom of our Lord and our King Jesus
Christ; His is the glory and the honour and the
power and the worship (προσκυνησις) to the age of
all ages. Amen.

Remember the disciple that wrote, Makarius, that
the Lord may give rest unto his miserable soul
(ψυχη). Amen.

II. THE TESTAMENT OF JACOB
(Cod. Copt, Vat. 61, f 178a)

THIS again also is the coming forth from the body
(σωμα) of our father the Patriarch (πατριαρχης) Jacob,
who is called Israel, on the twenty-eighth day of the
month Mesore, in the peace (εἰρηνη) of God Amen.

Now (δε) it came to pass when the days of our
beloved father Jacob the Patriarch, the son of Isaac,
the son of Abraham, drew nigh that he should come
forth from the body (σωμα), and (δε) the God-loving
Jacob was advanced in days, the Lord sent unto him
Michael the archangel (ἀρχαγγελος) ; and he said
unto him Israel, my beloved and thou good root,
write thy words of instruction for thy sons, and
establish for them thy testament (διαθηκη), and
take care for thine household; for the time is come
that thou shalt go unto thy fathers and have joy with
them for ever. But (δε) the God-loving Jacob,
when (f. 178b) he heard these words from the angel
(ἀγγελος), answered and spake unto him on this wise :
My lord (now it was his custom (συνηθεια) daily to
speak with angels (ἀγγελος)), he spake unto him
on this wise : May the will of the Lord be done.

And God blessed our father Jacob He put him
in a solitary place whither he could retire (ἀναχωρειν),
making his prayers (εὐχη) unto God day and night .

angels (ἀγγελος) came to seek after him, watching over him, saving him, giving him strength in all things. God blessed him; and his people (λαος) multiplied in the land of Egypt exceedingly For (γαρ) in the time when he came down into Egypt unto Joseph his son, his eyes were dimmed through much weeping and grief for Joseph his son, but (δε) when he came down into Egypt, he saw clear, when he beheld the face of Joseph his son And Jacob Israel cast himself down upon his face, upon the neck (f. 179a) of Joseph his son, he worshipped him, weeping and saying Now let me die, because I have seen thy face once more and thou still (ἐτι) livest, O my beloved; and (δε) Joseph was king over the whole of Egypt. Jacob dwelt in the land of Goshen seventeen years; he became exceeding old, full[1] of days, he kept all the commandments (ἐντολη) and the fear of the Lord and his eyes were dimmed so that he saw no man, because of his exceeding old age

He lifted up his eyes unto the light of the angel (ἀγγελος) which spake with him, having the likeness and the face (προσωπον) of his father Isaac, he was afraid and troubled The angel (ἀγγελος) said unto him Be not afraid, Jacob I am the angel (ἀγγελος) that have walked with thee since thy childhood. I chose thee, that thou shouldst receive the blessing of Isaac they father and Rebecca thy mother. I am with thee, O Israel, in every (f. 179b) thing that thou doest and every thing that thou hast seen. It is I that delivered thee out of the hand of Laban when

---

[1] Lit " being perfected, completed in his days "

he pursued after thee, I gave thee all his possessions (χρημα). I blessed thee, and all thy wives, and thy children, and all thy beasts. It is I again that delivered thee from the hands of Esau. It is I again that showed thee the way into the land of Egypt, O Israel, I have made thee to spread out exceedingly. Blessed is thy father Abraham, because he became a friend of God on high through his hospitality. Blessed is thy father Isaac that begat thee, because his sacrifice (θυσια) was made perfect, pleasing unto God. Blessed art thou also, O Jacob, because thou didst see God face to face, and thou didst gaze upon (θεωρειν) the host (παρεμβολη) of the angels (αγγελος) of God on high Thou didst see the ladder set up upon the earth, with its head stretching unto heaven; (f. 180a) thou didst see also the Lord standing upon the head thereof in power unspeakable, thou didst cry aloud, saying: This is the house of God, and this is the gate (πυλη) of heaven. Blessed art thou, because thou hast found strength in God, and been mighty among men; now therefore be not troubled, O beloved of God. Blessed art thou, O Israel, and blessed is all thy seed (σπερμα), for ye shall be called Patriarchs (πατριαρχης) until the consummation (συντελεια) of this age (αιων); for (γαρ) verily ye are my people (λαος), and ye are the root of the servants of God. Blessed is every people (εθνος) that shall emulate thy holiness and thy virtues (αρετη) and thy righteousness (δικαιοσυνη) and thy good doings (πραξις) Blessed is the man that shall keep the remembrance of you on your honourable feast. Blessed is he that

shall do a deed of charity (ἀγαπη) in your name, or
give a cup of water unto a man, (f 180b) or bring a
perfect offering (προσφορα) unto your holy place
(τοπος) or any holy place (τοπος) in your name, or
give hospitality unto a stranger, or go to visit the
sick, or comfort an orphan (ὀρφανος), or clothe one
that is naked in your name; he shall lack no good
thing (ἀγαθον) in the world (κοσμος) [and he shall
gain][1] in the age (αἰων) also that is to come life
eternal. And (δε) more still for him that shall write
your life with its labours, or shall write it with his
hands, or read it with attention, together with him
that shall hear it with faith and confirmation of their
heart, and him that shall emulate your doing; for
they shall be forgiven all their sins, and they shall
be a gift (χαριζεσθαι) unto you in the kingdom of
the heavens. Now then arise, that thou mayest
be taken from labour (f. 181a) and sorrow unto
eternal repose, and thou shalt be brought unto rest
(ἀναπαυσις) unceasing and repose unfailing and light
unsetting, and joy and gladness and spiritual
(πνευματικος) pleasure (εὐφροσυνη). Now therefore charge thy words unto thy sons; and peace
(εἰρηνη) be with thee, for I must go unto Him that
sent me.

Now (δε) when he had thus spoken unto him,
the angel (ἀγγελος) went back (-ἀναχωρειν) away
from him in peace (εἰρηνη) up to the heavens, while
he looked after him And (δε) they that were in
the house heard him confessing (-ἐξομολογεισθαι)

---

[1] A couple of words of some such meaning as this seem to
have dropped out of the text.

the Lord, giving praise unto Him with blessings
And all his sons were gathered together unto him,
from the smallest to the greatest, all weeping and
being heavy at heart, saying : He departeth and
leaveth us.   And they would say unto him : O our
beloved father, what (f. 181b) shall we do, for we are
sojourners in a strange land?   Jacob said unto
them : Be not afraid; for (γαρ) God appeared unto
me in Mesopotamia, saying . I am the God of thy
fathers.   Be not afraid, I am with thee for ever,
and thy seed for ever that shall come after thee.
The land whereon thou standest, I will give it to thee
and thy seed for ever.   And again He said unto me :
Be not afraid to go down into Egypt; I will go with
thee down into Egypt, so that I may make thee to
multiply, and thy seed to flourish for ever, and
Joseph to lay his hands upon thine eyes.   And thy
people (λαος) shall multiply exceedingly in Egypt;
then they shall return unto Me in this place, and I
will do good unto them for thy sake.   Now therefore shall ye remove from this place.

(f. 182a) Now (δε) after this the days of Jacob
Israel drew nigh that he should come forth from the
body.   He called Joseph; he spake unto him after
this fashion · If I have found grace in thy sight,
then put thy blessed hand upon my thigh, and swear
unto me an oath in the sight of the Lord, to lay my
body (σωμα) in the sepulchre of my fathers.   But
(δε) Joseph said unto him : I will do according to
thy word, O my beloved father.   His father said
unto him : I will that thou swear   And (δε) Joseph
swore unto Jacob his father according to (κατα)

these words, to take his body (σωμα) unto the sepulchre of his fathers   And Jacob bowed himself [1] upon the neck of his son.

Now (δε) after these things, one sought for Joseph, saying : Behold, thy father is troubled. He took his two sons, Ephraim and Manasseh; he came unto Israel his father. When Israel saw them, he said unto Joseph ˙ Who are these of thine, O my son? (f 182b) Joseph said unto Jacob Israel his father . These are my sons which God gave me in the land of my lowliness. Israel said ˙ Bring them nigh unto me. Now (δε) the eyes of Israel were darkened through his exceeding old age, so that he could not see clear. And he brought them nigh unto him; he kissed them. When Israel had embraced them, he said : God shall add to thy seed. And Joseph made his two sons, Ephraim and Manasseh, bow down before him upon the ground. Joseph brought Manasseh under his right hand and Ephraim under his left hand. Israel changed his hands; he laid his right hand upon the head of Ephraim and his left hand upon the head of Manasseh   And he blessed them , he gave them their inheritance (κληρος), saying : (f. 183a) God, before whom my fathers were pleasing, Abraham and Isaac, the God which fed me from my childhood unto this day; the angel which redeemed me from all my tribulations (θλιψις), bless these lads that are my sons, that have my name named upon them and the name of my holy

---

[1] Lit " worshipped "   The Coptic word occurs several times in these " Testaments," and means something between " showed reverence to " and " made an inclination before."

H

fathers Abraham and Isaac. They shall increase and multiply; they shall become a great nation (λαος) upon the earth. Afterward Israel said unto Joseph. I shall die; and ye shall return again unto the land of your fathers, and God shall be with you Lo and behold, thou hast received a blessing above thy brethren, for (γαρ) I have taken the Amorites with my bow and my sword.

Jacob called all his sons, he said unto them · Come ye all together unto me, that I may tell you that what shall befall you, and again that which shall be-(f. 183b)-fall each one of you in the last days All the sons of Israel were gathered together unto him, from the least to the greatest. Jacob Israel answered and said unto his sons : Hear, ye sons of Jacob, hearken unto Israel your father, from Reuben my first-born unto Benjamin. He told them what should become of the twelve sons according to their names and their tribes (φυλη) in the blessing of heaven. Then was all the multitude of men silent, that he might repose a little while. He was taken up to the heavens, so that he might walk through the places of repose. And behold a multitude of tormentors (τιμωριστης) came out, each of them different in appearance, ready to torment (τιμωρειν) the sinners, namely, the whoremongers (πορνος), and the harlots (πορνη), and the effeminate (μαλακος), and them that defile themselves with men, (f. 184a) and the adulterers and them who have destroyed the creature (πλασμα) of God, and the sorcerers (μαγος), and the poisoners (φαρμακος); and them that do violence, and the servers of idols (ειδωλον), and the ıdlers, and the slanderers, and the double-tongued. In short (ἁπλῶς), for every sın whereof we have spoken, there ıs a great punıshment (κολασις), the fire that ıs not quenched, the place where there shall be weeping and gnashıng of teeth and the worm that sleepeth not. And ıt ıs a fearful thıng when thou art brought before the judge (κριτης), and ıt ıs a fearful thıng to come ınto the hands of the lıvıng God Woe unto all sınful men, for whom these tortures (βασανος) and these tormentors (τιμωριστης) are made ready. And again after these thıngs I was taken up, he showed me the place whereın my fathers were, Abraham and my father Isaac, whıch was all lıght, and they were full of lıfe and joy ın the kıngdom (f. 184b) of the heavens, ın the beloved cıty (πολις). And he showed me all the places of repose, and all the good things (ἀγαθον) made ready for the just, and the thıngs whıch eye hath not seen nor (οὐδε) ear heard, nor have they come unto the heart of man : these thıngs whıch God hath made ready for them that shall love Hım and do Hıs wıll upon earth, ıf they shall have made an end well (καλως) doıng Hıs wıll

After these thıngs Jacob saıd unto hıs sons . Lo and behold I am to be taken away and laıd wıth my people (λαος) Lay my body (σωμα) wıth my people (λαος) ın the double (διπλουν) sepulchre ın the field of Ephron the Hıttıte, whereın they burıed Abraham and Sarah hıs wıfe; whereın they burıed Isaac, in the pathway of the field ; wıth the sepulchre that ıs thereın whıch was purchased from the chıldren of Heth (f 185a) And (δε) when Jacob had made an end of saying these things, he drew up his feet upon the bed, he came forth from the body (σωμα) like unto all men. And the Lord came from heaven, and Michael and Gabriel went with him, and multitudes of legions (λεγεων) of angels (ἀγγελος), singing (-ὑμνος) before His face. They received the soul (ψυχη) of Jacob Israel into abodes (σκηνη) of light with his holy fathers, Abraham and Isaac Now (δε) these are the years of the life of Jacob Israel the Patriarch (πατριαρχης) Joseph set him before Pharaoh when he was an hundred and thirty years old, and other seventeen years did he live in Egypt, all these make an hundred and forty and seven years He fell asleep in a green old age, being perfect in every virtue (ἀρετη) and spiritual (πνευματικον) grace together : he gave praise unto God in all his ways, in the peace of God Amen

(f 185b) Joseph fell upon his father : he kissed[1] him, weeping for him. And (δε) Joseph commanded his servants that were embalmers, saying : Embalm my father well (καλως), after the manner of (κατα) the Egyptians. They spent forty days embalming Israel, and when they had finished the forty days of the embalming of Israel, they spent other eighty days mourning for him. Now (δε) when the days of the mourning of Pharaoh were ended, wherein he wept for Jacob because of his love for Joseph, Joseph spake with the great ones of Pharaoh saying unto them on this wise · If I have found grace in your eyes, speak for me unto Pharaoh the king, saying. My father

---

[1] I have here translated " kissed " because it is the word used in Gen. l 1, from which this passage is taken

made me swear, when he was about to come forth from the body (σωμα), saying, Bury my body (σωμα) in the sepulchre of my fathers, in the land of Canaan, (f 186a) now let him command me that I may bury my father there, and come again. Pharaoh the king spake unto Joseph the wise, saying . Go in peace (εἰρηνη) and bury thy father, according to (κατα) the oath which he made thee swear Take with thee the chariots (ἁρμα) and the cars and all the great ones of my kingdom, and whomever thou shalt require (-αἰτειν) from among my servants Joseph worshipped God before Pharaoh; he went from him. Joseph went up to bury his father; there went with him all the servants of Pharaoh, and the elders of Egypt, and all the house of Joseph, and his brethren, and all the house of Israel And there went up with him the chariots (ἁρμα) and the horsemen (ἱππευς); the host (παρεμβολη) became exceeding great. (f. 186b) And (δε) they stayed at the threshing-floor of Gadad which is upon the bank beyond Jordan : they mourned him there with a great and very sore mourning · and they made a mourning for him for seven days. They that dwelt in the lower land heard the mourning that was made at the threshing-floor of Gadad, they said : This grievous mourning is of the Egyptians. Unto this very day they call that place : The mourning of the Egyptians They carried Israel and buried him in the land of Canaan in the double sepulchre which Abraham bought for the price [1] (κτησις) of silver of Ephron the Hittite before Mamre. And (δε) Joseph returned into

[1] Lit " possession."

Egypt, and his brethren with him, and the host (παρεμβολη) of the house of Pharaoh. Joseph lived after the death (f 187a) of his father for many more years, being a king in Egypt But (δε) Jacob Israel died, and was laid with his people (λαος).

Behold now (μεν) we have told you these things for your assurance as to the coming forth from the body (σωμα) of our father the Patriarch (πατριαρχης) Jacob Israel, up to (προς) the measure which we could reach, seeing that it is written in the spiritual scriptures (γραφη) of God and the ancient (ἀρχαιος) compositions (συνταγμα) of our holy fathers the Apostles, even I,[1] Athanasius your father. If ye desire to know the establishment of this testament (διαθηκη) of the Patriarch (πατριαρχης) Jacob, take unto you the Genesis (γενεσις) of the prophet (προφητης) Moses the lawgiver (νομοθετης) and read therein, your mind (νους) shall receive light, ye shall find these things and more written concerning it.[2] Ye shall find God and His angels, (f 187b) God[3] being their friend while they were still in the body (σωμα), and speaking with them many times; in many passages of the scripture (γραφη) And again that He spake in many passages in the scripture with the Patriarch Jacob, saying I will bless thy seed like the stars of the heaven. And again Jacob was speaking with Joseph his son, saying My God

---

[1] I do not know whether it is really grammatically possible to consider this nominative in apposition with the plural nominatives at the beginning of the sentence, if not, one must supply with Andersson some lost verb with the sense " I have found ..."

[2] i e the " establishment " of the Testament

[3] I have repeated this word to show that the following participles (" being " and " speaking ") are in the singular.

appeared unto me in the land of Canaan, at Luz.
He blessed me, saying   I will bless thee, and make
thee multiply, and make peoples (λaos) and nations
($\epsilon\theta\nu os$) spring from thee , I will give this land unto thy
seed ($\sigma\pi\epsilon\rho\mu a$) after thee for an everlasting possession

Lo therefore ($o\check{v}\nu$), O my beloved, we have heard
these things concerning our fathers the Patriarchs;
let us emulate therefore ($o\check{v}\nu$) their doings ($\pi\rho a\xi\iota s$),
and their virtues ($\dot{a}\rho\epsilon\tau\eta$), and their love of God,
(f. 188a) and their love of men, and their hospitality,
so that ($\iota\nu a$) we may be worthy to become sons unto
them in the kingdom of the heavens , so that ($\iota\nu a$)
they may pray for us unto God, that ($\iota\nu a$) He may
deliver us from the punishments ($\kappa o\lambda a\sigma\iota s$) which are
in Hell, even those which the holy Patriarch Jacob
rehearsed in his words full of all sweetness, when
he was instructing his sons concerning the punish-
ments ($\kappa o\lambda a\sigma\iota s$), calling them the sword of the Lord
God.   These are the river of fire that is prepared,
making great waves for the sinners and for them that
have defiled themselves   These are the things which
the Patriarch ($\pi a\tau\rho\iota a\rho\chi\eta s$) Jacob revealed when he
was instructing the rest of his sons, so that ($\iota\nu a$) they
who love learning might listen and do that which is
good for all time, and love one another, and love
charity ($\dot{a}\gamma a\pi\eta$) and pity , for pity is praised above
judgement, and charity ($\dot{a}\gamma a\pi\eta$) covereth a multitude
of sins; (f 188b) and again, he that hath pity upon
the poor lendeth on usury unto God.

Now therefore, my sons, let us not fail[1] in prayer

---

[1] This word is missing in the Coptic text. It must have been
a verb with some such meaning.

and fasting (νηστεια), and remain ye in expectation,
for these are the things that drive away (-διωκειν)
the devils (δαιμων)   My sons, keep yourselves from
fornication (πορνεια), and wrath, and adultery, and
every evil thing, but (δε) especially violence and
blasphemy and thieving, for there is no violence that
shall inherit (-κληρονομειν) the kingdom of the
heavens; nor (ουδε) shall any whoremonger (πορνος),
nor (ουδε) effeminate (μαλακος), nor (ουδε) he that
defiles himself with men, nor (ουδε) blasphemer,
nor (ουδε) covetous, nor (ουδε) idolater, nor (ουδε)
curser, nor (ουδε) impure person, or in short (απλως)
of any of those that we have declared unto you, that
shall inherit (-κληρονομειν) the kingdom of God.
My sons, glorify the saints, for it is they who pray for
you that your seed (σπερμα) may multiply, (f 189a)
and that ye may inherit (-κληρονομειν) the earth in
an everlasting inheritance (κληρονομια)   My sons,
be hospitable, that ye may obtain the portion of
our father Abraham, the great Patriarch (πατριαρχης).
My sons, love the poor, that as thou doest unto the
poor here, so may God give thee the bread of life for
ever in the heavens, unto the end, he that shall give
a poor man to eat of the bread that is here, God shall
give him to eat from the tree of life.   Clothe the poor
man that is naked here upon earth, that He may put
upon thee a robe (στολη) of glory in the heavens, and
that thou mayest become a son of our holy fathers
the Patriarchs (πατριαρχης) Abraham and Isaac and
Jacob in the heavens for ever.   Have a care unto the
word of God here and remember the saints that
they may write their counsels (υπομνημα) and their

hymns (ὕμνος) which give comfort to them that hear
them, so that (ἵνα) they may write thy name (f. 189b)
also in the book of life in the heavens, and number
thee with the number of His saints that have pleased
Him in their generation (γενεα) and now take their
place (χωρευειν) with the angels (ἀγγελος) in the
place (χωρα) of the living. For we are keeping the
remembrance of the saints, our fathers the Patriarchs
(πατριαρχης) at (κατα) this season year by (κατα) year.
Our father Abraham the Patriarch (πατριαρχης) on
the twenty-eighth day of Mesore. Again, our father
Isaac the Patriarch (πατριαρχης) on the twenty-eighth
day of Mesore. And (δε) again, our father Jacob on
the twenty-eighth day of this same month Mesore,
even as (κατα) we have found it written in the ancient
(ἀρχαιος) compositions (συνταγμα) of our holy fathers
that were pleasing unto God. Through their supplications and their prayers may it happen unto us all
together to obtain their part (μερος) and their inheritance (κληρος) in the kingdom of our Lord and our
God and our Saviour (σωτηρ) Jesus Christ Through
Him is . . [1] the glory of the Father with Him, and
the Holy Ghost, the giver of life, now and always
and for ever. Amen.

Remember me, that God may forgive me all my
sins, and give me understanding, and give me rest
without sin Amen.

---

[1] A word or two seem to have dropped out of the text their
nature can be seen from the similar conclusion of the Coptic
text of the *Testament of Abraham*.

ADDITIONAL NOTE

P 30, NOTE 3 —The following description of the Angel of
Death is given in T. B. *'Abodah zarah* 20b · *It is said of the Angel
of Death that he is altogether full of eyes   At the time of the sick
man's departure he [the Angel] takes his stand above the place of
his [the sick man's] head, with his sword drawn in his hand, and
a drop of poison suspended on it   When the sick man sees it he
shudders, and opens his mouth, and it [the poison-drop] is injected
into his mouth , through it he dies, through it he becomes putrid,
through it his countenance becomes livid*

INDEXES

I —PASSAGES OF SCRIPTURE REFERRED TO

II —LITERATURE OUTSIDE THE BIBLE

III —NAMES AND SUBJECTS

CPSIA information can be obtained
at www.ICGtesting.com
Printed in the USA
LVHW011823180723
752687LV00005B/225